W9-BLF-795

Ethnic
Violence

OTHER BOOKS OF RELATED INTEREST

OPPOSING VIEWPOINTS SERIES
Africa
America's Victims
The Breakup of the Soviet Union
Central America
Discrimination
Hate Groups
Human Rights
Islam
The Middle East
Terrorism
The Third World
War
Weapons of Mass Destruction

CURRENT CONTROVERSIES SERIES
Hate Crimes
Interventionism
Nationalism and Ethnic Conflict
Racism
Urban Terrorism

AT ISSUE SERIES
Anti-Semitism
Ethnic Conflict
The United Nations
U.S. Policy Toward China

Ethnic Violence

Myra H. Immell, *Book Editor*

David L. Bender, *Publisher*
Bruno Leone, *Executive Editor*
Bonnie Szumski, *Editorial Director*
David M. Haugen, *Managing Editor*
Brenda Stalcup, *Series Editor*

Contemporary Issues
Companion

Greenhaven Press, Inc., San Diego, CA

Library of Congress Cataloging-in-Publication Data

Ethnic violence / Myra H. Immell, book editor
　　p.　　cm. — (Contemporary issues companion)
　　Includes bibliographical references and index.
　　ISBN 0-7377-0165-X (alk. paper). —
ISBN 0-7377-0164-1 (pbk. : alk. paper)
　　1. Political violence. 2. Ethnic relations—Political aspects. 3. Race relations. 4. Human rights. I. Immell, Myra. II. Series.
JC328.6.E875　2000
305.8—dc21　　　　　　　　　　　　　　　　　　99-36834
　　　　　　　　　　　　　　　　　　　　　　　　　　CIP

©2000 by Greenhaven Press, Inc.
P.O. Box 289009, San Diego, CA 92198-9009

Printed in the U.S.A.

CONTENTS

FOREWORD

In the news, on the streets, and in neighborhoods, individuals are confronted with a variety of social problems. Such problems may affect people directly: A young woman may struggle with depression, suspect a friend of having bulimia, or watch a loved one battle cancer. And even the issues that do not directly affect her private life—such as religious cults, domestic violence, or legalized gambling—still impact the larger society in which she lives. Discovering and analyzing the complexities of issues that encompass communal and societal realms as well as the world of personal experience is a valuable educational goal in the modern world.

Effectively addressing social problems requires familiarity with a constantly changing stream of data. Becoming well informed about today's controversies is an intricate process that often involves reading myriad primary and secondary sources, analyzing political debates, weighing various experts' opinions—even listening to first-hand accounts of those directly affected by the issue. For students and general observers, this can be a daunting task because of the sheer volume of information available in books, periodicals, on the evening news, and on the Internet. Researching the consequences of legalized gambling, for example, might entail sifting through congressional testimony on gambling's societal effects, examining private studies on Indian gaming, perusing numerous websites devoted to Internet betting, and reading essays written by lottery winners as well as interviews with recovering compulsive gamblers. Obtaining valuable information can be time-consuming—since it often requires researchers to pore over numerous documents and commentaries before discovering a source relevant to their particular investigation.

Greenhaven's Contemporary Issues Companion series seeks to assist this process of research by providing readers with useful and pertinent information about today's complex issues. Each volume in this anthology series focuses on a topic of current interest, presenting informative and thought-provoking selections written from a wide variety of viewpoints. The readings selected by the editors include such diverse sources as personal accounts and case studies, pertinent factual and statistical articles, and relevant commentaries and overviews. This diversity of sources and views, found in every Contemporary Issues Companion, offers readers a broad perspective in one convenient volume.

In addition, each title in the Contemporary Issues Companion series is designed especially for young adults. The selections included in every volume are chosen for their accessibility and are expertly edited in consideration of both the reading and comprehension levels of the audience. The structure of the anthologies also enhances accessibility. An introductory essay places each issue in context and provides helpful facts such as historical background or current statistics and legislation that pertain to the topic. The chapters that follow organize the material and focus on specific aspects of the book's topic. Every essay is introduced by a brief summary of its main points and biographical information about the author. These summaries aid in comprehension and can also serve to direct readers to material of immediate interest and need. Finally, a comprehensive index allows readers to efficiently scan and locate content.

The Contemporary Issues Companion series is an ideal launching point for research on a particular topic. Each anthology in the series is composed of readings taken from an extensive gamut of resources, including periodicals, newspapers, books, government documents, the publications of private and public organizations, and Internet websites. In these volumes, readers will find factual support suitable for use in reports, debates, speeches, and research papers. The anthologies also facilitate further research, featuring a book and periodical bibliography and a list of organizations to contact for additional information.

A perfect resource for both students and the general reader, Greenhaven's Contemporary Issues Companion series is sure to be a valued source of current, readable information on social problems that interest young adults. It is the editors' hope that readers will find the Contemporary Issues Companion series useful as a starting point to formulate their own opinions about and answers to the complex issues of the present day.

INTRODUCTION

In recent years, ethnic conflict and violence seem to have suddenly erupted in nations across the globe. In Rwanda, the former Yugoslavia, Pakistan, Indonesia, and many other countries, ethnic violence has become a fact of life. But ethnic conflict and violence are not new phenomena. They represent a long-term global problem that over time has resulted in the deaths of millions of people, leaving millions of others homeless. The first large-scale act of ethnic violence in the modern world took place at the beginning of the twentieth century, when the Turks committed genocide (a systematic and planned annihilation) against the Armenians. The massive genocide of World War II, known as the Holocaust, took the lives of millions of people—primarily Jews, but also Gypsies, Poles, Slavs, and other ethnic groups deemed inferior by the German Nazis.

For several decades after World War II, ethnic violence seemed to lessen in its frequency and intensity. By the early 1990s, however, a number of civil wars between different ethnicities—often horrifying in the extreme violence committed against civilians—made the problem of ethnic violence one of pressing international concern. After the fall of the Soviet Union in 1991, the former communist nation of Yugoslavia started splitting apart along ethnic lines, periodically breaking out into bloody civil wars. The 1994 civil war in the African nation of Rwanda pitted one ethnicity against another, resulting in the death of more than 1 million Rwandans and making refugees out of another 3 million people. These two examples of recent ethnic warfare are the most well known, but many other ethnic conflicts have recently occurred or are ongoing in countries throughout the world.

Ethnic violence has become an all-too-common fact of modern life. According to numerous experts, ethnic conflict is one of the primary causes of the wars that have begun in recent decades. Wars based on ethnic conflict frequently prove difficult to resolve and tend to last a long time, possibly dragging on for generations. Typically, the cost in lives is extremely high. For instance, in 1998, *Scientific American* reported that since 1945 more than 15 million people have been killed in ethnic conflicts.

What causes these violent conflicts? Generally, ethnic violence originates in the intense dislike or hatred that members of one ethnic group have for those of another ethnic group. This hatred may be rooted deeply in ancient history; there may have been centuries of mistrust, misunderstanding, and violence between certain ethnic groups. If the two ethnic groups have religious differences, this may intensify their conflict. Ethnic conflict can also be exacerbated if the two ethnic groups are of different races, as with whites and blacks in

9

South Africa and the United States. In addition, such hatred may stem from one group's feelings of superiority over the other and a tendency to blame the other group for everything that goes wrong. One case in point is the Nazis' attitude toward Jews before and during World War II. For centuries, there had been a climate of distrust between the Christians and the Jews of Europe. The Nazis built on this by claiming that the German people were of the Aryan race and therefore superior to the Jews, who were of Semitic origin. The Nazis purposely fostered ethnic hatred against the Jews and then set out to systematically annihilate them.

However, these feelings of being different from and superior to another ethnic group do not in and of themselves lead to violent conflict. Some other factor usually comes into play, such as disputes between the ethnic groups over territory or control of the nation's government. The breakdown of the existing social or political order can also unleash ethnic warfare, especially in the case of the breakup of multinational states such as the Soviet Union. In the not-too-distant past, people tended to identify themselves foremost by their nationality, their political citizenship. For example, although Yugoslavia was made up of several different ethnic groups, these people primarily identified themselves as Yugoslavs. As the nation began to fall apart, the Yugoslav people became more and more likely to base their identities on their ethnicity—the combination of cultural factors that bind people together as a permanent group. Instead of considering themselves Yugoslavs, they began to identify themselves as Serbs, Croats, Albanians, and so forth. In situations such as this, each group makes its own claim to territory and seeks political dominance or autonomy. Hostile feelings grow and fester; neighbors watch each other nervously and some eventually take sides; and, before long, violence erupts.

Some experts believe that ethnic violence has increased considerably during the 1990s. A primary reason for this increase, they contend, is the end of multiethnic empires—especially the Soviet Union, which many regard as having been the last existing empire. These empires would typically attempt to disregard or erase ethnic diversity, requiring their citizens to learn one language and discouraging religious or cultural differences. The Soviet Union consisted of a variety of ethnic groups, but according to U.S. ambassador John McDonald, the Soviets "kept the lid on conflict within their empire" by making sure that citizens were not given the freedom to express their ethnicity or call for more tolerance of ethnic diversity. With the demise of the Soviet empire, McDonald argues, the situation reversed itself: "Today there's nobody to keep the lid on." Ethnic groups who had been repressed took immediate advantage of the breakup of the Soviet Union to declare independence and set up their own governments—and to settle old grudges or new disputes with other ethnic groups.

In the view of these experts, another reason for the apparent increase in ethnic violence is the ability of ethnic groups to operate in ways they could not as recently as ten years ago. Whereas political and military force were not options for most ethnic groups in the past, say these experts, in recent years they have become more available—and some ethnic groups do not hesitate to use them. The Israeli-Arab conflict, for example, has been going on for several decades. When Israel first became a state in 1948, the Israelis did not have the strong political structure or military power that they have today. The Palestinians have also gained more support, larger numbers, and greater access to Arab governments and leaders than previously. Such developments have made it more likely that ethnic violence will occur.

Experts also indicate that a third possible reason for the increase in ethnic violence is that the international community is ill-prepared to deal with ethnic conflicts. McDonald states that "no organization and no officially recognized mechanism [exist] to deal with ethnic violence." The United Nations in particular has been reluctant to step in when ethnic conflict breaks out between members of the same nation, since traditionally it has not gotten involved in civil wars or internal conflicts. When one nation invades another, such as when Iraq invaded Kuwait, the United Nations can step in—and often does. NATO and the world powers also have interceded in order to end such wars. But most ethnic conflict takes place within national borders and—so long as the concept of national sovereignty still exists—outside help generally is not forthcoming. Many experts recommend that some sort of international policy needs to be established whereby ethnic violence can be prevented or ended, instead of being allowed to escalate.

While most historians, educators, and scientists agree that a major cause of ethnic violence is the dislike or hatred of one group for another, not all believe that ethnic identities are ancient and unchanging. Some experts contend that ethnic identities are modern creations. According to these experts, the empires or colonial governments that ruled many countries until recently manufactured ethnicities by arbitrarily classifying and grouping the native peoples. For instance, a number of scholars believe that the two warring ethnic groups of Rwanda, the Hutu and the Tutsi, are actually far more similar than different in their language, culture, and other elements of ethnic identification. These experts argue that the Hutu and Tutsi "ethnic" groups were created relatively recently by the European colonials who once ruled the Rwandan people. The colonists encouraged one group to feel superior to the other, and both groups to stereotype and fear each other. The tensions that exist between the Hutu and the Tutsi are very real, these experts claim, but they are rooted in recent events rather than ancient history or actual ethnic diversity. Other authorities take issue with the assumption that identifying with a particular ethnic group motivates people to persecute and kill. Most people would gladly live together in harmony, they insist, if their leaders did not generate the fear and hate that ultimately lead to ethnic violence.

The selections included in *Ethnic Violence: Contemporary Issues Companion* will not provide readers with easy explanations or simple solutions for ethnic conflict. They will, however, make the reader more aware of some major incidents of ethnic violence that have afflicted various nations from the time of the Armenian genocide to the present day. The authors of the selections include research scientists, academicians, government officials, and humanitarian and human rights organizations seeking to prevent future ethnic conflict. They provide insights into the factors that cause and fuel ethnic conflict, as well as examining the devastating effects that ethnic violence can have on individuals, ethnic groups, nations, and the global community as a whole.

CHAPTER 1

ETHNIC VIOLENCE:
CAUSES AND CURES

Contemporary Issues
Companion

THE ROOTS OF ETHNIC VIOLENCE

Patrick A. McGuire

Patrick A. McGuire is a staff member of the *APA Monitor*, the magazine of the American Psychological Association. In the following selection, McGuire reports on a number of theories put forth by a group of scholars—psychologists, sociologists, political scientists, and historians—about the roots of ethnic conflicts. According to McGuire, these scholars agree that there is a link between group identity, emotion, and ethnic violence. People identify with a certain group when their feelings and emotions match those experienced by the group as a whole. In time, the group begins to think of itself as better than other groups, thereby boosting the self-esteem of the group's members. The group's members then conclude that other groups are keeping them from achieving what they want. The end result is violence, with one group pitted against another.

In New Guinea, wars often break out because pigs belonging to one group stray into the garden of another. This, according to psychologist Clark McCauley, PhD, of Bryn Mawr College, was an interesting discovery made by a colleague, but not as interesting as the idea that many times when pigs got into another group's garden, no war was waged at all.

In the cases where the offended group did not pursue war against its neighbors, members fought bitterly amongst themselves, essentially over the level of 'moral violation' they felt had been caused by the errant pigs.

It highlighted, said McCauley at a conference in July 1998 in Londonderry, Northern Ireland, on ethnopolitical warfare, a driving force behind such conflict. 'It's emotion—the willingness to sacrifice personal safety, even life, in the interest of group conflict,' he said.

McCauley's ideas were presented to a group of about 50 prominent scholars in the fields of psychology, sociology, political science and history. Many elaborated on their life's work studying ethnopolitical warfare in a specific hostile region of the world. From those experiences they were able to draw conclusions about the psychological underpinnings of such conflict that applied around the world.

For example, Anthony Oberschall, PhD, of the University of North Carolina, in speaking about his experiences in Bosnia, talked of in-group fighting that sounded similar to the in-fighting over pigs in New Guinea.

'In ethnic competition,' he said, 'the conflict within groups is almost as important as between groups.'

Group Identity, Emotion, and Violence

During the week-long conference, theorists were in much agreement about the link between group identity, emotion and violence.

'By group identification I mean feeling positive and negative outcomes of a group as your own,' said McCauley.

'I don't mean empathy. We've all had the experience of knowing a group where something bad has happened to them. They are angry, we're sad. There, our emotions don't match.'

In the context of ethnopolitical warfare, McCauley said, group identification 'means expanding the boundaries of what an individual cares about. It goes past the boundaries of narrow self-interest.'

Ervin Staub, PhD, of the University of Massachusetts, defines ethnopolitical violence as 'violence based on any differentiation by group.' And, he said, such violence tends to evolve toward the ultimate crime of genocide along 'a continuum of destruction' that begins simply enough with what he called 'difficult conditions of life.'

'Fundamental human needs are frustrated,' he said. 'There develops a need for control, of positive identity—a need for connection.'

Out of such needs, he said, come 'the beginning of restlessness and a demand for more.' People begin turning to groups for their identity. 'The psychological and social process turns one group against another,' said Staub. The result, he said, 'is an ideology based on antagonism.' People elevate their own group to gain a better sense of themselves, while at the same time devaluing another group.

'What makes this destructive is that one group is usually identified as an enemy that stands in the way of the fulfillment of their position,' said Staub. 'They view the other group as mortal enemies, it becomes part of their group's identity. And it has a vision of a better world in which the other is eliminated.'

A Conceptual Framework

Two dangers of studying ethnopolitical warfare, said Kenneth Jowitt, PhD, of the University of California at Berkeley, are the tendency to either generalize that all ethnic conflicts are the same, or to fall into the trap of deciding that the case you happen to be studying is incredibly unique. Which is why, he said, he developed a conceptual framework for organizing material when looking at conflicts.

In his framework there are three types of conflict and violence, with three types of identity and entity:

• The corporate or 'barricaded' model, which is dogmatic and hysterical about defending the righteousness of its identity. He cited the Catholic Church during the Middle Ages as an example.

• The individual or 'bounded' model. The opposite of the barricaded mentality, it emphasizes resemblance, not differences. 'A bounded role is being a Democrat or a Republican, but you're both Americans.' Whereas, being identified as 'Orange' or 'Green' in Northern Ireland is built on differences.

• Ego identities, or the 'frontier' model. They are marked by lethal violence, he said 'but the violence is ghetto-like. It doesn't have much in the way of ideological rationale.' The hallmark of a frontier setting is a weak state such as Russia today, Bosnia, Somalia, Albania and Afghanistan. The danger, he said, is that unchecked frontier models can generate into an extremist, super-ethnic version of the barricaded model, backed by power. That, he said, is how Lenin and Stalin came to power after the Russian Civil War. It is also how Nazi Germany developed.

FOUR CATEGORIES OF ETHNIC CONFLICTS

United Nations Research Institute for Social Development

According to the United Nations Research Institute for Social Development (UNRISD), the dynamics of all ethnic conflicts are not the same. Instead, they fall into four distinct categories: separatist movements, competition for state resources, struggles of indigenous peoples, and minority rights. These four categories are described in the following selection. In the view of UNRISD, almost all ethnic conflicts worldwide can be placed into one of the four categories or into a combination of these categories. Based in Geneva, Switzerland, UNRISD is an autonomous agency that works through a large network of national research centers to conduct research on the social dimensions of problems currently affecting international development.

Ethnic differences do not always translate into open conflicts—and some of those that do are not threatening to the social and political order as mutually accepted mechanisms exist to regulate them. Others are not only difficult to manage, but they sometimes turn violent, create widespread instability and lead to loss of life. Although many ethnic conflicts erupt spontaneously, most need political entrepreneurs or mobilizers, a network of organizations and a discourse (or set of principles or ideas) to activate them. Ethnic mobilizers always compete for the loyalties of their putative followers. All individuals in a group may not subscribe to an ethnic cause, either because they value other relationships or their commitment to the conflict is fuzzy. Ethnicity may overlap with social class or status in deeply divided societies where structures of discrimination block social mobility for specific ethnic groups.

In most other cases the link between ethnicity and class is not that direct. Instead, ethnicity may be used to mask class interests or prevent social groups in different ethnic formations from organizing along common class lines. Such complexities in ethnic consciousness help to underscore the point that, when a conflict develops, there are often two or more organizations competing, sometimes violently, for the loyalty of an ethnic group.

Reprinted, with permission, from "The Search for Identity: Ethnicity, Religion, and Political Violence," published by the United Nations Research Institute for Social Development, Geneva, Switzerland, at www.unrisd.org/engindex/publ/list/op/op6/op6-03.htm.

Four categories of ethnic conflicts can be distinguished, based on a group's objectives, its orientation towards the state and the way it defines the discourse of its struggle. These types of conflicts are those that are separatist in nature; those that are concerned with distributing advantages within a single state structure; those that focus on the rights of indigenous peoples; and those that seek to protect the rights of minorities in societies where one group constitutes the majority population. The majority of ethnic conflicts can be placed into one of these categories, or a combination of them.

Separatist Movements

Separatist types of conflicts can take two forms: secession and internal autonomy. What determines a group's preference for one is not always clear—as the cases of the Sudan People's Liberation Army (SPLA) and the Liberation Tigers of Tamil Eelam (LTTE) demonstrate. The peoples of southern Sudan and the Tamils of Sri Lanka face similar types of discrimination from the dominant groups in their two countries—Arabs in the case of the Sudan and Sinhalas in Sri Lanka. Southern Sudanese have been fighting against Arabization, Islamization, state control of southern lands and resources and discrimination in public sector jobs. The LTTE has also waged a bitter war against the use of Sinhalese as the official language in Sri Lanka, the adoption of Buddhism as the state religion, and discrimination in educational opportunities, job allocation and government appointments. Yet, despite what would appear to be a more systematic and racist form of domination in the Sudan compared to what obtains in Sri Lanka, the SPLA has been fighting for autonomy and reform of the central state, and not for secession. The LTTE, on the other hand, has been uncompromising in its demand for a separate Tamil state.

A key condition for separatism is the availability of territory that an aggrieved group can claim as its own and defend. Such territory is usually difficult to obtain because it may span several states. "Kurdistan", for example, covers parts of Iran, Iraq, Syria and Turkey, and leaders of these states are reluctant to cede territory to the Kurds. Alternatively, the territory may contain some of the peoples of the dominant group from whom an aggrieved group seeks to secede, as is the case with the ongoing conflict between Croats, Muslims and Serbs in Bosnia. Secessionist conflicts resonate with highly charged discourses of "us" versus "them" and a fanatical commitment to achieve the desired separation. But not all separatist conflicts are pursued through armed struggle. Some, like those in Quebec, Scotland and Wales, are waged through constitutional means, and may be moderated by electoral cycles, becoming intense in one period and slack in another. And not all secessionist conflicts lead to separation, as the cases of Biafra in Nigeria, Papua and Bougainville in Papua New Guinea, the Casamance in Senegal and the Basques in Spain demonstrate.

Competition for State Resources

Most ethnic conflicts in the world are of the second type, where ethnic groups pursue their claims within an existing state structure. The aim is not to create an alternative state but to either capture the existing state or improve access to it. Frustration of this goal may lead, however, to demands for secession or autonomy. Indeed, several separatist movements start from a position of competition for the existing state and graduate into fully fledged separatist movements. Conflicts based on competition for the state can be either bi-polar or multi-polar. In bi-polar conflicts there are roughly two groups struggling for control of the state. Examples include Hutus and Tutsis in Burundi and Rwanda, Fijians and Indians in Fiji, Africans and Indians in Guyana and Trinidad, and Chinese and Malays in Malaysia. Under conditions of bi-polarity, the scope for flexibility in bargaining and in the formation of alliances may be highly constrained as each group believes the other has a hegemonic plan which it could easily enact because of the two-way nature of all contests. Conflicts may be moderated where one of the groups accepts a subordinate position in politics in exchange for higher benefits in the economy or in other domains. An example is Malaysia, where the Chinese seem to have ceded political control of the country to the indigenous Malays in exchange for continued Chinese dominance of the economy. Where such accommodation cannot be reached, conflicts can lead to blood baths as has happened in Burundi and Rwanda.

Under conditions of multi-polarity, ethnic groups may not always have permanent enemies, only "permanent" interests, as they may be forced to make alliances in order to achieve their objectives. In a typical multi-ethnic setting, as in Nigeria, for example, domination or exclusion is often achieved by one central group acting in alliance with other groups either on a regional basis or based on other criteria such as religion and loosely defined ideologies. The Igbos of Nigeria lost their war of secession partly because most of the ethnic groups in the oil regions of the east that were to form part of Biafra did not see themselves as part of an eastern coalition. They were contemptuous of secession, which they felt would strengthen Igbo domination of the region. All Nigerian governments since independence have been ethnic coalition governments, although such coalitions have not included every group or have included some groups unequally. It is also possible for multi-polar conflicts to become bi-polar, especially where there are two main ethnic groups around which smaller ones coalesce. Sometimes, bi-polarity can take local forms as two dominant groups fight for control of local lands, services and governments. A number of conflicts in countries with large populations and ethnic groups tend to take this form. In Nigeria, local communal land conflicts intensified in the late 1980s and early 1990s with the creation of new states by the federal government. In Hyderabad and Karachi,

Sindhis have been locked in conflict with Urdus, or Mohajirs as they are called, for control of the regional government and economic opportunities in the two Pakistani cities. The Sindhis claim these cities as their own, but they have been dominated by the Urdus since they left India in 1947 to settle in Pakistan as the founders of the new Muslim state.

Patronage plays a key role in the dynamics of both bi-polar and multi-polar conflicts. Political entrepreneurs rely on an ethnic clientele to access resources from the state, and may use such connections to deflect censure of their activities in public life. They nurture support from wide social networks such as church organizations, mosques, shrines, welfare associations, and unions of workers, students and professionals, although the nature of support may vary in each case. In cases where interest groups are trans-ethnic, unions may refuse to support ethnic-based governments or political parties in their defence of workplace interests. Ethnic entrepreneurs may be able to mobilize individual workers, students and professionals to support their political programmes outside of union structures, however. In Nigeria, workers are more likely to support their unions in industrial disputes with governments or opposition parties, than they are likely to do on issues relating to national politics, where ethnicity becomes a major variable. Where interest groups are uni-ethnic—such as in Fiji, Guyana, Malaysia and Trinidad—unions may simply become extensions of the ethnic political parties or movements. Ethnic mobilizers are generally well versed in the cultures and traditions of their societies, offer services and protection to some of those in need, and pose as the custodians of community interests. Where competition is fluid, the discourse for mobilization may not always be cast in non-negotiable terms as deals may have to be made and alliances redefined. However, the bargaining could be just as violent as in separatist conflicts.

Struggles of Indigenous Peoples

Conflicts of the third type relate to the rights of indigenous peoples and revolve around land issues and the protection of indigenous cultures and languages. The development of the world market and European migration into foreign lands has had a devastating effect on indigenous peoples in the Americas and Australasia. Many indigenous groups have been exterminated, their lands have been confiscated, and their cultures and languages have been degraded. The majority of those who have survived occupy the lowest stratum of the social structure in the countries where they live. They tend to be poorly educated, less well catered for in the social sector, grossly underrepresented in the political system, and are either landless or possess only insecure tenured rights to land. . . .

The way of life of indigenous peoples is intimately linked to the land. First, as farmers, hunters or gatherers, they need land for their basic survival. Second, land is also important for their cultural, spiritual and psychological well-being. In contemporary times, land that indigenous groups still possess has come under threat from the state and transnational companies as forest and mineral resources become profitable in the world market. The struggles of indigenous groups are primarily, therefore, about land and the preservation of their cultures. They have campaigned to retrieve parts of the lands they lost historically to Europeans, as is the case in Australia, Canada, New Zealand and the United States, and for the right to govern themselves in those lands as autonomous peoples using their own laws, traditions and institutions. In many countries of Latin America, such as Brazil, Mexico and Nicaragua, indigenous peoples' protests are part of their wider struggles for land redistribution, economic upliftment, civic rights and the protection of forests against the forces of modernization. Recently, forest dwellers in the Amazon region of Brazil, in collaboration with mestizo rubber tappers, have been engaged in a struggle to protect their forests against logging companies, corrupt government officials and land speculators; the Miskito Indians have been resisting forced incorporation into the Sandinistas' national development project in Nicaragua; and Indian peasant guerrillas—Zapatistas—in the province of Chiapas have risen up against the Mexican state demanding land and provincial social reforms.

Minority Rights

Minority rights conflicts constitute the fourth category; these are of two types. First, some conflicts over minority rights are a consequence of the creation of nation states in Europe, which left a large number of individuals residing in states not bearing the name of their ethnicity or nationality: Hungarians in Romania, Serbia, Slovakia and Ukraine; Germans in the Czech Republic, Hungary, Poland and Slovakia; and Russians in the new states that have been created out of the USSR. Several smaller groups that live in existing nation states do not have a parent nationality that has a state: the three million Gypsies scattered across most East European countries; the Basques in Spain and France; Valacs, Cincaris and Arumanians in the Balkans; the Saamis in Norway; the Lapps in Sweden, Finland and northern Russia; and the 41 different ethnic groups that live in present-day Russia. Minority rights struggles focus either on the rights of minority groups to form autonomous governments in the territories where they constitute a majority, or on special measures to protect their culture, language and religion where they do not form a majority, as well as on equal treatment in the allocation of national resources and government offices.

The second type of minority rights conflicts relates to recent migrations to Western Europe. Examples of this type can be observed in Belgium, France, Germany, Italy, the Netherlands, Switzerland and the United Kingdom. In this second type, immigrants do not seek to claim or defend any territorial rights. As in the first type, however, they are concerned with issues of legal status, discriminatory practices in the economy and government policies, the right to practice their culture and religion, and the regulation of ethnic and racial violence. Until very recently, most states were ambivalent towards immigrant populations, especially as the bulk of these were initially brought in as "guest workers" who were expected to return home when the host population no longer needed their labour. The idea that immigrants are not likely to return to their country of origin and should thus be seen as minority groups with identities of their own has developed only recently. Even so, most states, especially France and Germany, have favoured assimilation of immigrants into the dominant culture as opposed to supporting immigrants' cultural traditions and their right to retain and practice them. This has been a major source of tension between host communities and immigrant groups, particularly Muslim Algerians in France, Muslim Turks in Germany, and Sikhs and Muslim Pakistanis in the United Kingdom, who tend to rely on their cultures to insert themselves into the new societies. Racist-inspired violence has been on the increase in many European cities and anti-immigrant and racist parties are gaining electoral strength in several European countries.

However, immigrants are also organizing to fight back and have gained footholds within established political parties and unions through the support of anti-racist movements among the host population as well. Although they have been successful in some areas of local government, it is precisely at those lower levels of government that anti-immigrant parties have also made large inroads.

PREVENTING GENOCIDE

Samuel Totten and William S. Parsons

Samuel Totten is a professor of curriculum and instruction at the University of Arkansas at Fayetteville. William S. Parsons is the chief of staff for the United States Holocaust Memorial Museum in Washington, D.C. In the following selection, Totten and Parsons write that, according to the United Nations, genocide involves committing very specific acts "with the intent to destroy, in whole or in part, a national, ethnical, racial, or religious group." In the authors' view, scholars and activists must take a more active role in documenting lesser-known genocides and must band together to effect positive change. Totten and Parsons also urge scholars, activists, and educators to make an all-out educational effort to "reach students in a way that has not been attempted" before concerning the issue of genocide.

Will the killing ever stop? Will the scourge of genocide ever be eradicated? Will humanity ever be wise enough to prevent the deaths of potential genocidal victims *before*, as Samuel Totten has written, they "become yet another set of statistics in the welter of statistics?"

These and similar thoughts weigh heavily on our minds as we write this essay. . . . How could they not? Daily broadcasts and reams of print journalism issue terrible news about the "ethnic cleansing" that took place in Bosnia-Herzegovina; the recent slaughter of hundreds of thousands of Tutsis and Tutsi sympathizers by Rwandan government forces and paramilitary extremists; the mass killings perpetrated in Burundi; the intransigence and resurgence of the Khmer Rouge in Cambodia; the hateful epithets and actions of neo-Nazis in Germany, the United States, and elsewhere; the incremental and insidious destruction of indigenous peoples' ways of life across the globe; and the ubiquitous deprivation of various peoples' human rights (which, at times, explode into genocidal actions). . . .

At times it is difficult not to be disheartened, especially when governments deny and distort the historical record of genocide and/or do too little or nothing at all when new genocides erupt across the globe. Indeed, at times it is difficult not to wonder whether all the scholar-

Excerpted from the Introduction by Samuel Totten and William S. Parsons to *Century of Genocide: Eyewitness Accounts and Critical Views*, edited by Samuel Totten, William S. Parsons, and Israel W. Charny. Reprinted by permission of Garland Publishing, Inc.

ship, all the words, and all the pledges to "Never Forget" are simply an anodyne to ease the pain of the survivors and soothe the consciences of those who deeply care about such tragedies but feel impotent to stanch the deadly violence now referred to as genocide. And at times it is difficult not to wonder whether those of us who hold out hope that genocide can, at a minimum, be halted early on are doing so more out of desperation than any sense of objectivity or reality. This is especially so in this century that some have deemed the "century of genocide.". . .

What Is Genocide?

Ever since Raphael Lemkin, a Polish Jewish émigré and noted scholar who taught law at Yale and Duke universities, coined the term *genocide* in 1944, there has been an ongoing, and often heated, debate about what constitutes the most "exact" and "useful" definition of genocide. To form the new term, Lemkin combined the Greek *genos* (race, tribe), and *cide* (killing). He went on to define genocide as

> . . . the coordinated plan of different actions aiming at the destruction of essential foundations of the life of national groups with the aim of annihilating the groups themselves. The objectives of such a plan would be the disintegration of the political and social institutions of culture, language, national feelings, religion, economic existence, of national groups and the destruction of the personal security, liberty, health, dignity, and even the lives of the individuals belonging to such groups. Genocide is directed against the national group as an entity, and the actions involved are directed against individuals, not in their individual capacity, but as members of the national group.

. . . After lengthy debate and ample compromise, on December 9, 1948, the United Nations adopted the Genocide Convention and in doing so defined genocide in the following manner:

> In the present Convention, genocide means any of the following acts committed with the intent to destroy, in whole or in part, a national, ethnical, racial, or religious group, as such:
>
> a. Killing members of the group;
> b. Causing serious bodily or mental harm to members of the group;
> c. Deliberately inflicting on the group conditions of life calculated to bring about its physical destruction in whole or in part;
> d. Imposing measures intended to prevent births within the group;

e. Forcibly transferring children of the group to another group.

Quite obviously, this definition is, at one and the same time, extremely broad *and* extremely narrow. As a result, it is not surprising that over the years many scholars have proposed alternative definitions of genocide. As of yet, "no generally accepted definition of genocide is available in the literature," write authors Frank Chalk and Kurt Jonassohn. This, of course, constitutes a serious problem, especially as it relates to the intervention in and prevention of genocide as well as the prosecution of cases that involve genocidal-like actions. It also complicates the work of scholars as they undertake the study of the preconditions, processes, and ramifications of genocide. . . .

A Lack of Scholarly Study

Despite the impediments and difficulties that scholars, activists, and others face in collecting eyewitness accounts of certain genocidal acts, it is still extremely disturbing that there has not been a concerted and collective effort by both the scholarly and activist communities to collect as many accounts as possible of the least-documented genocides in the twentieth century. While not wishing to appear cynical, it seems that by not assisting those who have largely remained voiceless, we—the scholars and the activists—have contributed to, rather than ameliorated, the problem. Instead of locating the survivors and other witnesses in order to "return" the voices to the voiceless, we have remained on the sidelines. . . .

The amount and quality of scholarly study of different genocidal acts has varied greatly over the years. More specifically, while the Holocaust is the most heavily documented and studied genocide in the history of humanity, other genocidal events suffer from a serious lack of scholarly examination.

There is a great need to continue the scholarly work that has been done in order to understand the processes that lead up to and eventuate in acts of genocide. . . .

Certain scholars *and* activists seem to have come to the conclusion that, if there is ever going to be any hope at all of stanching genocidal actions, then they (and not governments) are going to have to be the catalyst behind such hope. And rightly so. Numerous times throughout the twentieth century no government (either individually or collectively) has taken it upon itself to address this issue nor to be proactive in this regard. Furthermore, as author-scholar Leo Kuper has trenchantly commented, "I assume that realistically, only a small contribution can be expected from the United Nations, at any rate in the immediate future." He goes on to say: "The performance of the United Nations in response to genocide is as negative as its performance on charges of political mass murder. There are the same evasions of responsibility and protection of offending governments and the same overriding concern for state interests and preoccupation with ideological and regional alliances."

We believe that a concerted effort needs to be made by as many scholars, activists, and nongovernmental bodies as possible to continue to study all aspects of genocide and human rights violations with an eye toward developing, as soon as possible, a genocide early warning system. It goes without saying that such a system will, at least at the outset and possibly for a good number of years, be quite rudimentary. So be it. Over time, it can be updated, overhauled, and strengthened with the aim of making it a more sophisticated and effective system.

The Power of a Collaborative Effort

Individually a person can only do so much to protest genocidal actions or to work on the behalf of oppressed individuals. Collectively, people have a much better chance of effecting positive change. Interestingly, it is estimated that today there are over 2,000 nongovernmental organizations working on various issues in the protection of international human rights. A small number of these organizations are working, in one way or another, on the issue of genocide. Many of them face a constant struggle to remain in existence; and this is due, in large part, to the limited resources they have at their disposal. As a result of this situation, both the focus of their efforts as well as their influence is limited. Certainly one key way for these organizations to gain more clout is to band together in order to complement and supplement one another's strengths as well as to act as a single body and to speak in one voice when addressing issues that they hold in common. . . .

Specifically, they need to begin to initiate campaigns against genocide with an eye toward influencing international public opinion as well as the decisions and actions of governmental organizations. They also need to establish themselves as a main source of documentation for investigating the perpetration of genocide. As it now stands, most individuals and organizations dealing with the issue of genocide are putting more time into working on the scholarly examination of genocide (including issues of intervention and prevention) rather than the actual intervention or prevention of genocide. . . .

It seems as if it would behoove the international community of scholars and activists working on the issue of genocide . . . to forge a working relationship, in which their work and the work of other nongovernmental organizations resulted in a strong and well-structured network which enabled them to combine forces in order to intervene and prevent genocide from taking place. Such an effort would constitute the inception of a strong, united critical mass working in concert toward the common goals of intervention and prevention. . . .

One of the key goals of such a network should be the development of a genocide early warning system whose purpose would be the early detection, intervention and, ultimately, prevention of genocide. . . .

An Early Warning System

While a completely operational genocide early warning system has yet to be developed, various components have been designed and implemented. For example, the work of International Alert is certainly in line with what needs to be done in order to detect and defuse possible situations that might culminate in genocide. On another note, Israel W. Charny, Director of the Institute on the Holocaust and Genocide (Jerusalem, Israel), has developed a major data base on all aspects (including preconditions) of genocide. Charny eventually wants to incorporate this data into a genocide early warning system.

Some of those who are dubious about the efficacy of such a system are concerned that unless the criteria for identifying the preconditions of genocide are clearly and exactly delineated early on the system might sound the alarm too often and consequently be disregarded due to its unreliability. It is our sense, though, that while an initial system may not work as well as anyone would like, to wait until such a system is totally reliable, or even, for example, just 50 percent reliable, is ludicrous. That said, we fully agree that there should be a genuine effort by those who develop and implement such a system to attempt to avoid "crying wolf" (i.e., claiming genocide) without ample research; . . . however, one of the most valuable contributions of a genocide early warning system will be to stave off situations that are moving toward genocide. Thus, even if a situation never explodes into genocide, the very fact, for example, that a team of conflict resolution specialists was sent to a trouble spot and managed to head off a massacre constitutes real progress. . . .

It is crucial for schools at all levels across the globe to teach their students about the causes and ramifications of genocide *as well as* each person's responsibility for acting in a moral manner when human rights infractions (including genocide) rear their ugly heads. As for the goal of Holocaust and genocide education, Israel Charny makes the perspicacious point that the goal "must be to make awareness of Holocaust and genocide part of human culture, so that more and more people are helped to grow out of killing and from being accomplices to killers, or from being bystanders who allow the torture and killing of others."

In essence, the sort of study that we advocate is one that . . . (1) engages the students in a study of accurate and in-depth information, ideas, and concepts, (2) contextualizes the history, (3) avoids simple answers to complex history, (4) and addresses issues of personal and societal responsibility both from a historical as well as a contemporary perspective.

Indeed, an all-out educational effort by scholars, activist organizations, and educators is needed. Working together, these three groups could produce outstanding curricular materials and reach students in a way that has not been attempted thus far, at least, in regard to the issue of genocide. . . .

We agree with Israel Charny, when he argues:

There needs to be a growing consensus on the part of human beings and organized society that penetrates the very basis of human culture that mass killing is unacceptable to civilized peoples, otherwise the prevailing momentum of historical experience will continue to confirm for generation after generation that genocide is a phenomenon of nature, like other disasters, and this view of the inevitability of genocide as an almost natural event will continue to justify it in the sense of convincing people that nothing can be done.

POWER SHARING: A STRATEGY TO PREVENT ETHNIC VIOLENCE

David A. Hamburg and Richard H. Solomon

In the following selection, David A. Hamburg and Richard H. Solomon point out that scholars and policymakers take different approaches to the issue of prevention of ethnic conflict and violence. However, according to Hamburg and Solomon, scholars and policymakers alike have come to view power sharing (an arrangement in which a nation's ethnic groups share equally in the political process) as a possible strategy to help prevent or end ethnic conflict and violence. To achieve a successful outcome, note the authors, the international community must become involved in volatile situations early on and must determine whether power sharing will work or if the antagonistic ethnic groups should separate into different nations. Hamburg is the cochair of the Carnegie Commission on Preventing Deadly Conflict, a Washington, D.C.–based commission that promotes new ideas to prevent and resolve warfare and violence. Solomon is the president of the United States Institute of Peace, a federally funded group in Washington that works to strengthen U.S. capabilities to promote the peaceful resolution of international conflicts.

The horrors of ethnic violence defy the imagination: Mass murder, rape, and wanton destruction of places of worship and universities carried out in some cases by people who had lived together peacefully. The world watches, seemingly helpless before the overwhelming force of hatred, and asks the inevitable question: "Couldn't someone have done something to prevent this?"

People who have devoted their lives to the study of ethnic conflict have sought answers to three components of this large question: What political conditions drive people to violence? What conditions allow people to settle their differences peacefully? What is the role of the international community when relations between groups become violent? Scholars have developed theories of ethnic conflict and of political institutions that can manage conflict and prevent the turn to

Adapted from the Foreword, by David A. Hamburg and Richard H. Solomon, to *Power Sharing and International Mediation in Ethnic Conflicts*, by Timothy D. Sisk (Washington, DC: Endowment of the United States Institute of Peace, 1996). Reprinted by permission of the publisher.

violence. They have extracted principles from a comprehensive study of past conflicts and moments where conflicts have been avoided, and they have presented their results to policymakers, hoping that the principles will guide foreign policy.

Yet, scholars notice that policymakers are often bored by these theoretical discussions. It is as if the scholar and policymaker are from two different cultures that thrive on different types of information. The scholar looks backward to find lessons; the policymaker looks ahead and often must improvise. The scholar can wait until all the facts are in; the policymaker cannot. The time horizon of the scholar may be years; the horizon of the policymaker, weeks, days, or hours. Scholars complain that policymakers' decisions are *ad hoc* and without a strategy informed by scholarship. Policymakers say that they often have no choice.

In a path-breaking study by Timothy Sisk, a Program Officer of the United States Institute of Peace, scholarship bridges the gap to policymaking. This is the first study to apply theories of democracy in multiethnic societies to international mediation aimed at preventing or stopping ethnic violence.

As Sisk's work notes, in deeply divided societies, where fear and ignorance are often driving forces of ethnic conflict, people tend to identify themselves by their ethnic group, the defining characteristic of the society. Such societies can ignite in violence especially when there is inequality among ethnic groups and discrimination against one or more groups, and when discrimination is reinforced by public policy.

To avoid violence political institutions must allow ethnic groups to participate in the political process and they must protect human rights. Rather than feeling fearful, ethnic groups will feel valued in such a society.

Power Sharing

Power-sharing arrangements can help lead divided societies toward a stable democracy and away from violence. Power sharing, appropriately structured, can encourage moderation and discourage extremism. It can be based on politicians' self-interest: They will do whatever is needed to get elected.

Power sharing can begin a profound movement of the society away from ethnicity as the strongest identifier. Coalitions may form along ethnic lines at the outset, but ideology or class may become more important. People feel strongly about ideology and class but they are less likely to defend themselves to the death than ethnic extremists. Power sharing has been successful in some societies but ineffective in others. It was essential in the peaceful change of government in South Africa. Without an agreement on transitional power sharing, the conflict over apartheid may not have been brought to an end, or a new round of killing may have occurred. Yet a power-sharing pact in Rwanda did not prevent genocide. . . .

All too often international mediation deals with the *process* of political change: Is it peaceful or violent? Mediators want to stop the violence by any means possible. The international community must be more involved in shaping the institutions that will ensure an enduring peace—the *outcomes* of political change. It needs to be involved early and address what may be the most important question: Is power sharing necessary, and possible, in this society or is separation a better course? Prescriptions are not possible because every situation is different. . . .

The Need for Democratization

In identifying preventive measures the Carnegie Commission on Preventing Deadly Conflict distinguishes between long-term structural tasks and immediate operational tasks to defuse a crisis. Structural prevention includes strategies to build intercommunal confidence, overcome deeply held mistrust, and restructure institutions that discriminate against certain ethnic groups. Democratization, which performs all these tasks, is a crucial element of structural prevention. . . . The established democracies, with so much relevant experience, can play essential catalyzing and sustaining roles to help countries negotiate the complicated and slow process of democratization. . . .

There will be ethnic conflicts in the future, conflicts that could easily become very violent. The critical question is whether such conflicts can be managed without resort to violence, and, ideally, through the structures of participatory democracy. An alert, active international community—with the close collaboration of scholars and policymakers—can help parties forestall a turn to violence by encouraging the adoption of an appropriately structured power-sharing agreement based on democratic principles.

ETHNIC VIOLENCE: FACT OR FICTION?

Yahya Sadowski

Yahya Sadowski is an associate professor at Johns Hopkins University's Paul H. Nitze School of Advanced International Studies in Washington, D.C. In the following selection, Sadowski lists six commonly held beliefs about ethnic conflicts and argues that each is flawed or wrong. For example, he cites the belief that ethnic conflict ripped apart the Soviet Union, which he maintains is historically inaccurate. Sadowski points out that ethnic conflicts generally result from, rather than cause, the collapse of states. The demise of the Soviet Union occurred because of political reasons rather than ethnic conflict, he concludes. Such misconceptions are harmful, Sadowski suggests, because they can lead to ineffective policies concerning ethnic violence.

The Number of Ethnic Conflicts Rose Dramatically at the End of the Cold War.

Nope. The idea that the number of ethnic conflicts has recently exploded, ushering us into a violent new era of ethnic "pandaemonium," is one of those optical illusions that round-the-clock and round-the-world television coverage has helped to create. Ethnic conflicts have consistently formed the vast majority of wars ever since the epoch of decolonization began to sweep the developing countries after 1945. Although the number of ethnic conflicts has continued to grow since the Cold War ended, it has done so at a slow and steady rate, remaining consistent with the overall trend of the last 50 years.

In 1990 and 1991, however, several new and highly visible ethnic conflicts erupted as a result of the dissolution of the Soviet Union and Yugoslavia. The clashes between the armies of Croatia, Serbia, and Slovenia, and the agonizing battle that pitted Bosnia's Croats, Muslims, and Serbs against each other, occurred on Europe's fringes, within easy reach of television cameras. The wars in Azerbaijan, Chechnya, Georgia, and Tajikistan, while more distant, were still impressive in the way that they humbled the remnants of the former Soviet colossus. Many observers mistook these wars for the start of a new trend. Some were so impressed that they began to reclassify conflicts

Reprinted, with permission, from "Think Again: Ethnic Conflict," by Yahya Sadowski, *Foreign Policy* 111 (Summer 1998). Copyright 1998 by the Carnegie Endowment for International Peace.

in Angola, Nicaragua, Peru, and Somalia—once seen as ideological or power struggles—as primarily ethnic conflicts. . . .

Indeed, the most striking trend in warfare during the 1990s has been its decline: The Stockholm International Peace Research Institute documented just 27 major armed conflicts (only one of which, India and Pakistan's slow-motion struggle over Kashmir, was an interstate war) in 1996, down from 33 such struggles in 1989. Once the Cold War ended, a long list of seemingly perennial struggles came to a halt: the Lebanese civil war, the Moro insurrection in the Philippines, regional clashes in Chad, the Eritrean secession and related battles in Ethiopia, the Sahrawi independence struggle, fratricide in South Africa, and the guerrilla wars in El Salvador and Nicaragua.

The majority of the wars that survive today are ethnic conflicts— but they are mostly persistent battles that have been simmering for decades. They include the (now possibly defunct) Irish Republican Army (IRA) insurgency in the United Kingdom; the struggle for Kurdish autonomy in Iran, Iraq, and Turkey; the Israeli-Palestinian tragedy; the Sri Lankan civil war; and long-standing regional insurrections in Burma, India, and Indonesia.

The Role of Ancient Tribal and Religious Rivalry

Most Ethnic Conflicts Are Rooted in Ancient Tribal or Religious Rivalries.

No way. The claim that ethnic conflicts have deep roots has long been a standard argument for not getting involved. According to political journalist Elizabeth Drew's famous account, President Bill Clinton in 1993 had intended to intervene in Bosnia until he read Robert Kaplan's book *Balkan Ghosts*, which, as Drew said, conveyed the notion that "these people had been killing each other in tribal and religious wars for centuries." But the reality is that most ethnic conflicts are expressions of "modern hate" and largely products of the twentieth century.

The case of Rwanda is typical. When Europeans first stumbled across it, most of the country was already united under a central monarchy whose inhabitants spoke the same language, shared the same cuisine and culture, and practiced the same religion. They were, however, divided into several castes. The largest group, the Hutus, were farmers. The ruling aristocracy, who collected tribute from all other groups, was recruited from the Tutsis, the caste of cattle herders. All groups supplied troops for their common king, and intermarriage was not unusual. Social mobility among castes was quite possible: A rich Hutu who purchased enough cattle could climb into the ranks of the Tutsi; an impoverished Tutsi could fall into the ranks of the Hutu. Anthropologists considered all castes to be members of a single "tribe," the Banyarwanda.

Then came the Belgians. Upon occupying the country after World War I, they transformed the system. Like many colonial powers, the

Belgians chose to rule through a local elite—the Tutsis were eager to collaborate in exchange for Belgian guarantees of their local power and for privileged access to modern education. Districts that had been under Hutu leadership were brought under Tutsi rule. Until 1929, about one-third of the chiefs in Rwanda had been Hutu, but then the Belgians decided to "streamline" the provincial administration by eliminating all non-Tutsi chiefs. In 1933, the Belgians issued mandatory identity cards to all Rwandans, eliminating fluid movement between castes and permanently fixing the identity of each individual, and his or her children, as either Hutu or Tutsi. As the colonial administration penetrated and grew more powerful, Belgian backing allowed the Tutsis to increase their exploitation of the Hutus to levels that would have been impossible in earlier times.

In the 1950s, the Belgians came under pressure from the United Nations to grant Rwanda independence. In preparation, Brussels began to accord the majority Hutus—the Tutsis constituted only 14 percent of the population—a share of political power and greater access to education. Although this policy alarmed the Tutsis, it did not come close to satisfying the Hutus: Both groups began to organize to defend their interests, and their confrontations became increasingly militant. . . . The era of modern communal violence began with the 1959 attack on a Hutu leader by Tutsi extremists; Hutus retaliated, and several hundred people were killed. This set in motion a cycle of violence that culminated in December 1963, when Hutus massacred 10,000 Tutsis and drove another 130,000–150,000 from the country. These tragedies laid the seeds for the genocide of 1994.

The late emergence of ethnic violence, such as in Rwanda, is the norm, not an exception. In Ceylon (Sri Lanka), riots that pitted Tamils against Sinhalese did not erupt until 1956. In Bosnia, Serbs and Croats coexisted with one another, and both claimed Muslims as members of their communities, until World War II—and peaceful relations resumed even after the bloodshed of that conflict. Turks and Kurds shared a common identity as Ottomans and wore the same uniforms during World War I; in fact, the first Kurdish revolt against Turkish rule was not recorded until 1925. Muslims and Jews in Palestine had no special history of intercommunal hatred (certainly nothing resembling European anti-Semitism) until the riots of 1921, when nascent Arab nationalism began to conflict with the burgeoning Zionist movement. Although Hindu-Muslim clashes had a long history in India, they were highly localized; it was only after 1880 that the contention between these two groups began to gel into large-scale, organized movements. Of course, the agitators in all these conflicts tend to dream up fancy historic pedigrees for their disputes. Bosnian Serbs imagine that they are fighting to avenge their defeat by the Ottoman Turks in 1389; Hutus declare that Tutsis have "always" treated them as subhumans; and IRA bombers attack their victims in the name of a nationalist tradition they claim has burned since the Dark Ages. But these mythologies of hatred are themselves largely recent inventions.

The Fall of the Soviet Union

Ethnic Conflict Was Powerful Enough to Rip Apart the USSR.

Yeah, right. The idea that the Soviet Union was destroyed by an explosion of ethnic atavism has been put forth by a number of influential thinkers. . . . But this theory is not only historically inaccurate, it has misleading policy implications. The collapse of states is more often the cause of ethnic conflicts rather than the result.

Prior to 1991, ethnic consciousness within the Soviet Union had only developed into mass nationalism in three regions: the Baltic states, Transcaucasia, and Russia itself. Russian nationalism posed no threat to Soviet rule. . . . In Transcaucasia, the Armenians and Georgians had developed potent national identities but were much more interested in pursuing local feuds (especially with Muslims) than in dismantling the Soviet Union. Only in the Baltic states, which had remained sovereign and independent until 1940, was powerful nationalist sentiment channeled directly against Moscow.

When the August 1991 coup paralyzed the Communist Party, the last threads holding the Soviet state together dissolved. Only then did rapid efforts to spread nationalism to other regions appear. In Belarus, Ukraine, and across Central Asia, the nomenklatura, searching for new instruments to legitimate their rule, began to embrace—and sometimes invent—nationalist mythologies. It was amidst this wave of post-Soviet nationalism that new or rekindled ethnic conflicts broke out in Chechnya, Moldova, Ukraine, and elsewhere. Yet even amid the chaos of state collapse, ethnonationalist movements remained weaker and less violent than many had expected. Despite the predictions of numerous pundits, revivalist Islamic movements only took root in a couple of places (Chechnya and Tajikistan). Relations between indigenous Turkic peoples and Russian immigrants across most of Central Asia remained civil.

Savagery and Genocide

Ethnic Conflicts Are More Savage and Genocidal Than Conventional Wars.

Wrong. Although this assumption is inaccurate, the truth is not much more comforting. There appears to be no consistent difference between ethnic and nonethnic wars in terms of their lethality. In fact, the percentage of civilians in the share of total casualties is rising for all types of warfare. . . .

Furthermore, ethnic wars are less likely to be associated with genocide than "conventional" wars. The worst genocides of modern times have not been targeted along primarily ethnic lines. Rather, the genocides within Afghanistan, Cambodia, China, the Soviet Union, and even, to a great extent, Indonesia and Uganda, have focused on liquidating political dissidents. . . .

Finally, some pundits have claimed that ethnic conflicts are more likely to be savage because they are often fought by irregular, or guerrilla, troops. In fact, (a) ethnic wars are usually fought by regular armies, and (b) regular armies are quite capable of vicious massacres. Contrary to the stereotypes played out on television, the worst killing in Bosnia did not occur where combatants were members of irregular militias. . . . The core of the Serb separatist forces consisted of highly disciplined troops that were seconded from the Yugoslav army and led by a spit-and-polish officer corps. It was precisely these units that made the massacres at Srebrenica possible: It required real organizational skill to take between 6,000 and 10,000 Bosnian troops prisoner, disarm and transport them to central locations, and systematically murder them and distribute their bodies among a network of carefully concealed mass graves. Similarly, the wave of ethnic cleansing that followed the seizure of northern and eastern Bosnia by the Serbs in 1991 was not the spontaneous work of crazed irregulars. Transporting the male Bosnian population to concentration camps at Omarska and elsewhere required the talents of men who knew how to coordinate military attacks, read railroad schedules, guard and (under-) supply large prison populations, and organize bus transport for expelling women and children.

The Impact of Globalization

Globalization Makes Ethnic Conflict More Likely.

Think again. The claim that globalization—the spread of consumer values, democratic institutions, and capitalist enterprise—aggravates ethnic and cultural violence is at the core of Samuel Huntington's "clash of civilizations" hypothesis. . . . Although this suggestion deserves further study, the early indications are that globalization plays no real role in spreading ethnic conflict and may actually inhibit it.

Despite the fears of cultural critics that the broad appeal of the television show *Baywatch* heralds a collapse of worldwide values, there is not much concrete evidence linking the outbreak of ethnic wars to the global spread of crude materialism via film, television, radio, and boombox. Denmark has just as many television sets as the former Yugoslavia but has not erupted into ethnic carnage or even mass immigrant bashing. Meanwhile, Burundi, sitting on the distant outskirts of the global village with only one television set for every 4,860 people, has witnessed some of the worst violence in this decade.

The spread of democratic values seems a slightly more plausible candidate as a trigger for ethnic violence: The recent progress of democracy in Albania, Armenia, Croatia, Georgia, Moldova, Russia, Serbia, and South Africa has been attended by ethnic feuding in each country. But this is an inconsistent trend. Some of the most savage internal conflicts of the post-Cold War period have occurred in societies that were growing less free, such as Egypt, India, Iran, and Peru. For that matter, many of the worst recent ethnic conflicts occurred in countries where the regime type was unstable and vacillated back and forth between more and less free forms. . . .

Investigating the impact of economic globalization leads to three surprises. First, the countries affected most by globalization—that is, those that have shown the greatest increase in international trade and benefited most significantly from foreign direct investment—are not the newly industrializing economies of East Asia and Latin America but the old industrial societies of Europe and North America. Second, ethnic conflicts are found, in some form or another, in every type of society: They are not concentrated among poor states, nor are they unusually common among countries experiencing economic globalization. Thus, the bad news is that ethnic conflicts do not disappear when societies "modernize."

The good news, however, lies in the third surprise: Ethnic conflicts are likely to be much less lethal in societies that are developed, economically open, and receptive to globalization. Ethnic battles in industrial and industrializing societies tend either to be argued civilly or at least limited to the political violence of marginal groups, such as the provisional IRA in the United Kingdom, Mohawk secessionists in Canada, or the Ku Klux Klan in the United States. The most gruesome ethnic wars are found in poorer societies—Afghanistan and Sudan, for example—where economic frustration reinforces political rage. It seems, therefore, that if economic globalization contributes to a country's prosperity, then it also dampens the level of ethnic violence there.

Ending the Fighting

Fanaticism Makes Ethnic Conflicts Harder to Terminate.

Not really. . . . Militarily, ethnic conflicts are not intrinsically different from any other type of combat. They can take on the form of guerrilla wars or conventional battles; they can be fought by determined and disciplined cadres or by poorly motivated slobs. How much military force will be required to end the fighting varies widely from one ethnic conflict to the next.

However, achieving a military victory and building a durable peace are two very different matters. Sealing the peace in ethnic conflicts may prove harder for political—not military—reasons. Ethnic conflicts are fought among neighbors, among people who live intermingled with one other, forced to share the same resources and institutions. When two states end a war, they may need only to agree to stop shooting and respect a mutual border. But in ethnic conflicts there are often no established borders to retreat behind. Sometimes, ethnic disputes can be resolved by drawing new borders—creating new states that allow the quarreling groups to live apart. Other times, they can be terminated by convincing the combatants that they must share power peaceably and learn to coexist. . . .

In either case, ending ethnic warfare often requires the expensive and delicate construction of new political institutions. Not only may this be more difficult than terminating a "normal" interstate war, it may also take much longer. Building truly effective states takes time. For this reason, ethnic wars whose participants are already organized into states or protostates are probably easier to bring to a conclusion than battles in regions where real states have yet to congeal.

CHAPTER 2

ETHNIC VIOLENCE IN THE TWENTIETH CENTURY: A HISTORICAL PERSPECTIVE

Contemporary Issues
Companion

THE ARMENIAN GENOCIDE

Rouben Adalian

Rouben Adalian is the director of the Armenian Institute in Washington, D.C. In the following essay, he describes the conflict between the Ottoman Turks and the Armenians that led to the Armenian genocide of 1915 to 1918. Adalian writes that the Turks had committed ethnic violence against the Armenians before, but he argues that certain features distinguish the genocide from the massacres of earlier years. According to Adalian, the earlier outbreaks of violence primarily targeted men, but during the genocide, women and children also were killed. Secondly, he relates, the Turks attempted to hide the genocide, moving the Armenians from their homes to remote locations to be killed so the general public and the international community would not realize what was happening. Adalian reveals that of two million Armenians, only five hundred thousand survived the genocide, and most of these survivors fled their homeland, never to return.

Between 1915 and 1918 the Ottoman Empire, ruled by Muslim Turks, carried out a policy to eliminate its Christian Armenian minority. This genocide was preceded by a series of massacres in 1894–1896 and in 1909, and was followed by another series of massacres beginning in 1920. By 1922 Armenians had been eradicated from their historic homeland.

There are at least two ways of looking at the Armenian experience in the final days of the Ottoman Empire. Some scholars regard the series of wholesale killings from the 1890s to the 1920s as evidence of a continuity in the deteriorating status of the Armenians in the Ottoman Empire. They maintain that, once initiated, the policy of exposing the Armenians to physical harm acquired its own momentum. Victimization escalated because it was not countermanded by prevailing outside pressure or attenuated by internal improvement and reconciliation. They argue that the process of alienation was embedded in the inequalities of the Ottoman system of government and that the massacres prepared the Ottoman society for genocide.

Other scholars point out that the brutalization of disaffected ele-

Excerpted from "The Armenian Genocide: Context and Legacy," by Rouben Adalian, *Social Education: The Official Journal of the National Council for the Social Studies,* February 1991. Reprinted with permission. (References in the original have been omitted from this reprint.)

ments by despotic regimes is a practice seen across the world. The repressive measures these governments use have the limited function of controlling social change and maintaining the system. In this frame of reference, genocide is viewed as a radical policy because it reaches for a profound alteration of the very nature of the state and society. These scholars emphasize the decisive character of the Armenian genocide and differentiate between the periodic exploitation and occasional terrorization of the Armenians and the finality of the deliberate policy to exterminate them and eliminate them from their homeland.

Like all empires, the Ottoman Empire was a multinational state. At one time it stretched from the gates of Vienna in the north to Mecca in the south. From the sixteenth century to its collapse following World War I, the Ottoman Empire included areas of historic Armenia. By the early part of the twentieth century, it was a much shrunken state confined mostly to the Middle East. Yet its rulers still governed over a heterogeneous society and maintained institutions that favored the Muslims, particularly those of Turkish background, and subordinated Christians and Jews as second-class citizens subject to a range of discriminatory laws and regulations imposed both by the state and its official religion, Islam.

The failure of the Ottoman system to prevent the further decline of the empire led to the overthrow of the government in 1908 by a group of reformists known as the Young Turks. Formally organized as the Committee of Union and Progress, the Young Turks decided to Turkify the multiethnic Ottoman society in order to preserve the Ottoman state from further disintegration and to obstruct the national aspirations of the various minorities. Resistance to this measure convinced them that the Christians, and especially the Armenians, could not be assimilated. When World War I broke out in 1914, the Young Turks saw it as an opportunity to rid the country of its Armenian population. They also envisioned the simultaneous conquest of an empire in the east, incorporating Turkish-speaking peoples in Iran, Russia, and Central Asia.

The defeat of the Ottomans in World War I and the discrediting of the Committee of Union and Progress led to the rise of the Turkish Nationalists. Their objective was to found a new and independent Turkish state. The Nationalists distanced themselves from the Ottoman government and rejected virtually all its policies, with the exception of the policy toward the Armenians. . . .

Sultan Abdul-Hamid II's Massacres

From 1894 to 1896, Sultan Abdul-Hamid II carried out a series of massacres of the Armenian population of the Ottoman Empire. The worst of the massacres occurred in 1895, resulting in the death of thousands of civilians (estimates run from 100,000 to 300,000) and leaving tens of thousands destitute. Most of those killed were men. In many towns, the central marketplace and other Armenian-owned businesses were destroyed, usually by conflagration. The killings were done during the day and were witnessed by the general public.

This kind of organized and systematic brutalization of the Armenian population pointed to the coordinating hand of the central authorities. Widespread violence erupted in towns and cities hundreds of miles apart over a matter of weeks in a country devoid of mass media. At a time when the sultan ruled absolutely, the evidence strongly implicated the head of state.

The massacres were meant to undermine the growth of Armenian nationalism by frightening the Armenians with the terrible consequences of dissent. The furor of the state was directed at the behavior and the aspirations of the Armenians. The sultan was alarmed by the increasing activity of Armenian political groups and wanted to curb their growth before they gained any more influence by spreading ideas about civil rights and autonomy. Abdul-Hamid took no account, however, of the real variation in Armenian political outlook, which ranged from reformism and constitutionalism to separatism. He hoped to wipe away the Armenians' increasing sense of national awareness. He also continued to exclude the Armenians, as he did most of his other subjects, from having a role in their own government, whether individually or communally. The sultan, however, did not contemplate depriving the Armenians of their existence as a people. Although there are similarities between Abdul-Hamid's policies and the measures taken by the Young Turks against the Armenians, there are also major distinctions.

Three Distinguishing Features

The measures implemented in 1915 affected the entire Armenian population, men, women, and children. They included massacres and deportations. As under the sultan, they targeted the able-bodied men for annihilation. The thousands of Armenian men conscripted into the Ottoman army were eliminated first. The rest of the adult population was then placed under arrest, taken out of town, and killed in remote locations.

The treatment of women was quite different. . . . Countless Armenian women lost their lives in transit. Before their tragic deaths, many suffered unspeakable cruelties, most often in the form of sexual abuse. Many girls and younger women were seized from their families and taken as slave-brides.

During the time of the sultan, Armenians were often given the choice of converting to Islam in order to save themselves from massacre. However, during the genocide years, this choice was usually not available. Few were given the opportunity to accept Islam as a way of avoiding deportations. Most Armenians were deported. Some lives were spared during deportation by random selection or involuntary conversion through abduction, enslavement, or the adoption of kid-napped and orphaned children.

A second distinguishing feature of the genocide was the killing of the Armenians in places out of sight of the general population. The deportations made resistance or escape difficult. Most important, the removal of Armenians from their native towns was a necessary condi-tion of maintaining as much secrecy about the genocide as possible. The Allies had warned the Ottoman government about taking arbi-trary measures against the Christian minorities. The transfer of the Armenian population, therefore, was, in appearance, a more justifi-able response in a time of war.

When the Ottomans entered World War I, they confined journalists to Istanbul, and since the main communications system, the tele-graph, was under government control, news from the interior was cen-sored. Nonetheless, the deportations made news as soon as they occurred, but news of the massacres was delayed because they were done in desolate regions away from places of habitation. Basically, this provided cover for the ultimate objective of destroying the Armenian population. Inevitably the massacres followed the deportations.

A third feature of the genocide was the state confiscation of Armenian goods and property. Apart from the killing, the massacres of 1895 and 1909 involved the looting and burning of Armenian neighborhoods and businesses. The objective was to strike at the financial strength of the Armenian community, which controlled a significant part of the Ottoman commerce. In 1915 the objective of the Young Turks was to plunder and confiscate all Armenian means of sustenance, thereby increasing the probability of extinction.

Unlike the looting associated with the massacres under Sultan Abdul-Hamid II, the assault against the Armenians in 1915 was marked by comparatively little property damage. Thus, the genocide effortlessly transferred the goods and assets—homes, farms, bank accounts, buildings, land, and personal wealth—of the Armenians to the Turks. Since the Young Turk Party controlled the government, the seizure of the property of the Armenians by the state placed local par-ty chiefs in powerful positions as financial brokers. This measure esca-lated the incentive for government officials to proceed thoroughly with the deportation of the Armenians.

The Young Turks did not rely as much on mob violence as the sul-tan had. They implemented the genocide as another military opera-tion during wartime. The agencies of government were put to use, and where they did not exist, they were created. The Young Turk Party functionaries issued the instructions. The army and local gendarmerie carried out the deportations. An agency was organized to impound the properties of the Armenians and to redistribute the goods. "Butch-er battalions" of convicts released from prisons were organized into killer units. The Young Turks tapped into the full capacity of the state to organize operations against all 2 million Armenian inhabitants of the Ottoman Empire, and did it swiftly and effectively. . . .

Technology and Mass Killings

Coordination of the massacres during the reign of Abdul-Hamid II, and of the deportations under the Young Turks, was made possible by the telegraph. Of all the instruments of the state government, the telegraph dramatically increased the power of key decision-makers over the rest of the population. The telegraph system allowed for the kind of centralization that heretofore was impossible. . . .

To expedite the transfer of Armenians living in proximity of the railways, orders were issued instructing regional authorities to transport Armenian deportees by train. Instructions were explicit to the point of ordering the Armenians to be packed to the maximum capacity in the cattle cars which were used for their transport. The determination of the government to complete this task is demonstrated by the deportation of the Armenians in European Turkey who were ferried across the Sea of Marmara to Anatolia and then placed on trains for transport to Syria.

The removal of Armenians from Anatolia and historic Armenia was carried out mostly through forced caravan marches or by the use of trains. Although a large portion of the Armenians survived the horrific conditions of the packed cattle cars, they were not able to endure the Syrian desert where they were to die of hunger and thirst. In contrast, the majority of the Armenians in the caravans never reached the killing centers in the Syrian desert; many were murdered by raiding groups of bandits or died from exposure to the scorching days and cold nights. Most of those who were able to endure the "death marches" could not survive the starvation, exhaustion, or the epidemics that spread death in the concentration camps of the Syrian desert.

A Legacy of Loss

All too often the discussion of genocide centers on the numbers killed and fails to consider the wider implications of uprooting entire populations. Genocides are cataclysmic for those who survive because they carry the memory of suffering and the realization of the unmitigated disaster of genocide. Genocides often produce results and create conditions that make it impossible to recover anything tangible from the society that was destroyed, let alone permit the subsequent repair of that society. . . .

In a single year, 1915, the Armenians were robbed of their 3000-year-old heritage. The desecration of churches, the burning of libraries, the ruination of towns and villages—all erased an ancient civilization. With the disappearance of the Armenians from their homeland, most of the symbols of their culture—schools, monasteries, artistic monuments, historical sites—were destroyed by the Ottoman government.

The Armenians saved only that which formed part of their collective memory. Their language, their songs, their poetry, and now their tragic destiny remained as part of their culture.

Beyond the terrible loss of life (1,500,000), and the severing of the connection between the Armenian people and their historic homeland, the Armenian genocide also resulted in the dispersion of the survivors. Disallowed from resettling in their former homes, as well as stateless and penniless, Armenians moved to any country that afforded refuge. Within a matter of a few decades Armenians were dispersed to every continent on the globe. The largest Armenian community is now found in the United States.

By the expulsion of the Armenians from those areas of the Ottoman Empire that eventually came to constitute the modern state of Turkey, the reconfiguration of Armenia took a paradoxical course. Whereas the genocide resulted in the death of Armenian society in the former Ottoman Empire, the flight of many Armenians across the border into Russian territory resulted in compressing part of the surviving Armenian population into the smaller section of historic Armenia ruled by the Russians. Out of that region was created the present country of Armenia, the smallest of the republics of the USSR.

The contrast on the two sides of that frontier spotlights the chilling record of genocide. Three and a half million Armenians live in Soviet Armenia. Not an Armenian can be found on the Turkish side of the border.

The Postwar Period

During the genocide, the leaders of the world were preoccupied with World War I. Some Armenians were rescued, some leaders decried what was happening, but the overall response was too little too late.

After the war, ample documentation of the genocide was made available and became the source of debate during postwar negotiations by the Allied Powers. It was during these negotiations for a peace treaty that the Western leaders had an opportunity to develop humanitarian policies and strategies that could have protected the Armenians from further persecution. Instead of creating conditions for the prevention of additional massacres, the Allies retreated to positions that only validated the success of ideological racialism. The failure at this juncture was catastrophic. Its consequences persist to this day.

With the defeat of their most important ally, Germany, the Ottomans signed an armistice, ending their fight with the Allies. The Committee of Union and Progress resigned from the government and in an effort to evade all culpability soon disbanded as a political organization. Although many of the Young Turk leaders, had fled the country, the new Ottoman government in Istanbul tried them in absentia for organizing and carrying out the deportations and massacres. A verdict of guilty was handed down for virtually all of them, but the sentencing could not be carried out.

The Istanbul government was weak and was compromised by the fact that the capital was under Allied occupation. Soon it lost the competence to govern the provinces, and finally capitulated in 1922 to the forces of Nationalist Turks who had formed a separate government based in Ankara. As for the sentences of the court against the Young Turk leaders, they were annulled. The criminals went free.

The postwar Ottoman government's policies toward the Armenians were largely benign. They desisted from further direct victimization, but rendered no assistance to the surviving Armenians to ease recovery from the consequences of their dislocation. Many Armenians returned to their former homes only to find them stripped of all furnishings, wrecked, or inhabited by new occupants. Their return also created resentment and new tensions between the Armenians, filled with anger at their mistreatment, and the Turks, who, because of their own great losses during the war, believed they had a right to keep the former properties of the Armenians. In the absence of the Ottoman government's intervention to assist the Armenians, this new hostility contributed to increasing popular support for the Nationalist movement.

Rise of the Turkish Nationalists

The armistice signed between the Allies and the Ottomans did not result in the surrender of Turkish arms. On the contrary, it only encouraged the drive for Turkish independence from Allied interference. Organized in 1919 under the leadership of an army officer named Mustafa Kemal, the Turkish Nationalist movement rejected the authority of the central government in Istanbul and sought to create an exclusively Turkish nation-state.

As the Kemalist armies brought more and more territory under their control, they also began to drive out the surviving remnants of the Armenian population. The Nationalist Turks did not resort to deportation as much as to measures designed to precipitate flight. In a number of towns with large concentrations of Armenian refugees, massacres again took a toll in the thousands. With the spread of news that the Nationalist forces were resorting to massacre, Armenians selected two courses of action. In a few places some decided to resist, only to be annihilated. Most chose to abandon their homes once again, and this time for good.

The massacres staged by the Nationalist forces so soon after the genocide underscored the extreme vulnerability of the Armenians. Allied troops stationed in the Middle East did not attempt to save lives. Even if the Turkish Nationalist forces could not have been stopped militarily, the failure to intervene signified the abandonment of the Armenians by the rest of the world.

Silence and Denial

For the Allies, their failure to protect the Armenians had been a major embarrassment, one worth forgetting. For the Turks, their secure resumption of sovereignty over Anatolia precluded any responsibility toward the Armenians in the form of reparations. All the preconditions were created for the cover-up of the Armenian genocide. The readiness of people on the whole to believe the position of legitimate governments meant that the suggestion that a genocide had occurred in the far reaches of Asia Minor would be made the object of historical revisionism and, soon enough, complete denial.

For almost fifty years, the Armenians virtually vanished from the consciousness of the world. Russian Armenia was Sovietized and made inaccessible. Diaspora Armenians were resigned to their fate. The silence of the world and the denials of the Turkish government only added to their ordeals.

The insecurities of life in diaspora further undermined the confidence of Armenians in their ability to hang on to some form of national existence. Constant dispersion, the threat of complete assimilation, and the humiliation of such total defeat and degradation contributed to their insecurities.

The abuse of their memory by denial was probably the most agonizing of their many tribulations. Memory, after all, was the last stronghold of the Armenian identity. The violation of this "sacred memory," as all survivors of the genocidal devastation come to enshrine the experience of traumatic death, has reverberated through Armenian society.

The persecution and later the abandonment of the Armenians left deep psychological scars among the survivors and their families. Sixty years after the genocide, a rage still simmered in the Armenian communities. Unexpectedly it exploded in a wave of terrorism. Clandestine Armenian groups, formed in the mid-1970s, sustained a campaign of political assassinations for a period of about ten years. They were responsible for killing at least two dozen Turkish diplomats.

Citing the Armenian genocide and Turkey's refusal to admit guilt as their justification, the terrorists were momentarily successful in obtaining publicity for their cause. They were unsuccessful in gaining broad-based support among Armenians or in wrenching any sort of admission from Turkey. Rather, the government of Turkey only increased the vehemence of its denial policy and embarked on a long-range plan to print and distribute a stream of publications questioning or disputing the occurrence of a genocide and distorting much of Armenian history.

Seeking International Understanding

During these years of great turmoil, other Armenians sought a more reasonable course for obtaining international understanding of their cause for remembrance. In the United States, commemorative resolutions were introduced in the House of Representatives, and in the Senate as recently as February 1990. These resolutions hoped to obtain formal U.S. acknowledgment of the Armenian genocide. But the intervening decades had seen a close alliance develop between the United States and Turkey. The State Department opposed passage of these resolutions. The Turkish government imposed sanctions on U.S. businesses and military installations in Turkey. In the final analysis the resolutions failed to muster the votes necessary for adoption.

Terrence Des Pres observed: "When modern states make way for geopolitical power plays, they are not above removing everything—nations, cultures, homelands—in their path. Great powers regularly demolish other peoples' claims to dignity and place, and sometimes, as we know, the outcome is genocide." These words are important in establishing the context in which peoples, Armenians and others, seek congressional resolutions, and perform other commemorative acts. It is part of the continuing struggle to reclaim dignity. The reluctance of governments to recognize past crimes points to the basic lack of motivation in the international community to confront the consequences of genocide.

Differing Attitudes and Policies

It is helpful to distinguish between the attitudes and policies of the Ottoman imperial government, the Young Turks, and the Nationalist movement. The Ottoman government, based on the principle of sectarian inequality, tapped into the forces of class antagonism and promoted the superiority of the dominant group over a disaffected minority. It made rudimentary use of technology in the implementation of its more lethal policies.

The Young Turks, based on proto-totalitarianism and chauvinism, justified their policies on ideological grounds. They marshaled the organizational and technological resources of the state to inflict death and trauma with sudden impact. When the Young Turks deported the Armenians from Anatolia and Armenia to Syria, the result was more than simply transferring part of the population from one area of the Ottoman Empire to another. The policy of exclusion placed Armenians outside the protection of the law. Yet, strangely, because they were still technically in the Ottoman Empire, there was the possibility of repatriation for the survivors given a change in government.

The Nationalists tapped the popular forces of Turkish society to fill the vacuum of power after World War I. Their policy vis-a-vis the Armenians was formulated on the basis of racial exclusivity. They made the decision that even the remaining Armenians were undesirable. Many unsuspecting Armenians returned home at the conclusion of the war in 1918. They had nowhere else to go. With the expulsion from Nationalist Turkey, an impenetrable political boundary finally descended between the Armenians and their former homes. The possibility of return was canceled.

Genocide contains the portents of the kind of destruction that can erase past and present. For the Armenian population of the former Ottoman Empire, it meant the loss of homeland and heritage, and a dispersion to the four corners of the earth. It also meant bearing the stigma of the statelessness.

At a time when global issues dominate the political agenda of most nations, the Armenian genocide underlines the grave risks of overlooking the problems of small peoples. We cannot ignore the cumulative effect of allowing state after state to resort to the brutal resolution of disagreements with their ethnic minorities. That the world chose to forget the Armenian genocide is also evidence of a serious defect in the system of nation-states which needs to be rectified. In this respect, the continued effort to cover up the Armenian genocide may hold the most important lesson of all. With the passage of time, memory fades. Because of a campaign of denial, distortion, and cover-up, the seeds of doubt are planted, and the meaning of the past is questioned and its lessons for the present are lost.

JEWISH GENOCIDE: THE HOLOCAUST

The Holocaust Memorial Center

The Holocaust Memorial Center is an organization dedicated to the preservation of the memory of the six million Jewish victims of the Holocaust of World War II. The following selection, taken from the center's web page, traces the rise to power in Germany of Adolf Hitler and the Nazis and describes their deliberate attempt to eradicate all the Jews of Europe. The article explains that the Germans believed they were of the Aryan race, which they considered ethnically superior to the Jews. The article recounts how the Nazis launched a massive propaganda machine to promote violent anti-Semitism, resulting in the torture and extermination of millions of European Jews.

The Holocaust (also called *Shoah* in Hebrew) refers to the period from January 30, 1933, when Adolf Hitler became chancellor of Germany, to May 8, 1945 (V-E Day), when the war in Europe ended. During this time, Jews in Europe were subjected to progressively harsh persecution that ultimately led to the murder of 6,000,000 Jews (1.5 million of these being children) and the destruction of 5,000 Jewish communities. These deaths represented 2/3rds of European Jewry and 1/3 of world Jewry. The Jews who died were not casualties of the fighting that ravaged Europe during World War II. Rather, they were the victims of Germany's deliberate and systematic attempt to annihilate the entire Jewish population of Europe, a plan Hitler called "the Final Solution" (*Endlosung*).

After its defeat in World War I, Germany was humiliated by the Versailles Treaty, which reduced its prewar territory, drastically reduced its armed forces, demanded the recognition of its guilt for the war, and stipulated it pay reparations to the allied powers. The German Empire destroyed, a new parliamentary government called the Weimar Republic was formed. The republic suffered from economic instability, which grew worse during the worldwide depression after the New York stock market crash in 1929. Massive inflation followed by very high unemployment heightened existing class and political differences and began to undermine the government.

Excerpted from "History of the Holocaust," by The Holocaust Memorial Center, 1998, published at www.holocaustcenter.com/historyof.shtml. Reprinted with permission.

On January 30, 1933, Adolf Hitler, leader of the National Socialist German Workers (Nazi) Party, was named chancellor by president Paul von Hindenburg after the Nazi party won a significant percentage of the vote in the elections of 1932. The Nazi Party had taken advantage of the political unrest in Germany to gain an electoral foothold. The Nazis incited clashes with the communists, whom many feared, disrupted the government with demonstrations, and conducted a vicious propaganda campaign against its political opponents, the weak Weimar government, and the Jews, whom the Nazis blamed for Germany's ills.

Anti-Jewish Propaganda

A major tool of the Nazis' propaganda assault was the weekly Nazi newspaper *Der Stürmer* (The Attacker). At the bottom of the front page of each issue, in bold letters, the paper proclaimed, "The Jews are our misfortune!" *Der Stürmer* also regularly featured cartoons of Jews in which they were caricaturized as hooked-nosed and ape-like. The influence of the newspaper was far reaching: by 1938 about a half million copies were distributed weekly.

Soon after he became chancellor, Hitler called for new elections in an effort to get full control of the Reichstag, the German parliament, for the Nazis. The Nazis used the government apparatus to terrorize the other parties. They arrested their leaders and banned their political meetings. . . .

When the elections were held, the Nazis . . . won a majority in the government.

The Nazis moved swiftly to consolidate their power into a dictatorship. On March 23, the Enabling Act was passed. It sanctioned Hitler's dictatorial efforts and legally enabled him to pursue them further. The Nazis marshalled their formidable propaganda machine to silence their critics. They also developed a sophisticated police and military force. . . .

With this police infrastructure in place, opponents of the Nazis were terrorized, beaten, or sent to one of the concentration camps the Germans built to incarcerate them. Dachau, just outside of Munich, was the first such camp built for political prisoners. Dachau's purpose changed over time and eventually became another brutal concentration camp for Jews.

By the end of 1934 Hitler was in absolute control of Germany and his campaign against the Jews in full swing. The Nazis claimed the Jews corrupted pure German culture with their "foreign" and "mongrel" influence. They portrayed the Jews as evil and cowardly, and Germans as hardworking, courageous, and honest. The Jews, the Nazis claimed, who were heavily represented in finance, commerce, the press, literature, theater, and the arts, had weakened Germany's economy and culture. The massive government-supported propagan-

da machine created a racial anti-Semitism. . . .
The superior race was the "Aryans," the Germans. . . .

The Plight of the Jews

The Nazis then combined their racial theories with the evolutionary theories of Charles Darwin to justify their treatment of the Jews. The Germans, as the strongest and fittest, were destined to rule, while the weak and racially adulterated Jews were doomed to extinction. Hitler began to restrict the Jews with legislation and terror, which entailed burning books written by Jews, removing Jews from their professions and public schools, confiscating their businesses and property, and excluding them from public events. The most infamous of the anti-Jewish legislation was the Nuremberg Laws, enacted on September 15, 1935. They formed the legal basis for the Jews' exclusion from German society and the progressively restrictive Jewish policies of the Germans.

Many Jews attempted to flee Germany and thousands succeeded by immigrating to such countries as Belgium, Czechoslovakia, England, France, and Holland. It was much more difficult to get out of Europe. Jews encountered stiff immigration quotas in most of the world's countries. Even if they obtained the necessary documents, they often had to wait months or years before leaving. Many families out of desperation sent their children first. . . .

On November 9–10, 1938, the attacks on the Jews became violent. Hershel Grynszpan, a 17-year-old Jewish boy distraught at the deportation of his family, shot Ernst von Rath, the third secretary in the German Embassy in Paris, who died on November 9. Nazi hooligans used this assassination as the pretext for instigating a night of destruction that is now known as Kristallnacht (the night of broken glass). They looted and destroyed Jewish homes and businesses and burned synagogues. Many Jews were beaten and killed; 30,000 Jews were arrested and sent to concentration camps.

Germany invaded Poland in September 1939, beginning World War II. Soon after, in 1940, the Nazis began establishing ghettos for the Jews of Poland. More than 10 percent of the Polish population was Jewish, numbering about three million. Jews were forcibly deported from their homes to live in crowded ghettos, isolated from the rest of society. This concentration of the Jewish population later aided the Nazis in their deportation of the Jews to the death camps. The ghettos lacked the necessary food, water, space, and sanitary facilities required by so many people living within their constricted boundaries. Many died from deprivation, starvation, and disease.

The "Final Solution"

In June 1941 Germany attacked the Soviet Union and began the "Final Solution." Four mobile killing groups were formed called Einsatzgruppen A, B, C, and D. Each group contained several commando units. The Einsatzgruppen gathered Jews town by town, marched them to huge pits dug earlier, stripped them, lined them up, and shot them with automatic weapons. The dead and dying would fall into the pits to be buried in mass graves. In the infamous Babi Yar massacre, near Kiev, 30,000–35,000 Jews were killed in two days. In addition to their operations in the Soviet Union, the Einsatzgruppen conducted mass murder in eastern Poland, Estonia, Lithuania, and Latvia. It is estimated that by the end of 1942, the Einsatzgruppen had murdered more than 1.3 million Jews.

On January 20, 1942, several top officials of the German government met to officially coordinate the military and civilian administrative branches of the Nazi system in order to organize a system of mass murder of the Jews. In the words of author Leni Yahil, this meeting, called the Wannsee Conference, "marked the beginning of the full-scale, comprehensive extermination operation [of the Jews] and laid the foundations for its organization, which started immediately after the conference ended."

While the Nazis murdered other national and ethnic groups, such as . . . Soviet prisoners of war, Polish intellectuals, and gypsies, only the Jews were marked for systematic and total annihilation. In the famed Nazi use of euphemism, they were marked for "Special Treatment" (*Sonderbehandlung*). "Special Treatment" meant that Jewish men, women, and children were to be methodically killed with poisonous gas. In the exacting records kept at the Auschwitz death camp, the cause of death of Jews who had been gassed was indicated by "SB," the first letters of the two words that form the German term for "Special Treatment."

By the spring of 1942, the Nazis had established six operating killing centers, or death camps, in Poland: Chelmno, Belzec, Sobibor, Treblinka, Majdanek, and Auschwitz. All were located near railway lines so that Jews could easily be transported to them on a daily basis. A vast system of camps (called Lagersystem) supported the death camps. The purpose of these camps varied: some were slave labor camps, some transit camps, others concentration camps and their sub-camps, and still others the notorious death camps. Some camps combined all of these functions or a few of them. All the camps were intolerably brutal. . . .

In nearly every country overrun by the Nazis, the Jews were forced to wear badges marking them as Jews. They were rounded up into ghettos or concentration camps, and then gradually transported to the killing centers. The death camps were essentially factories for murdering Jews. The Germans shipped thousands of Jews to them each day. Within a few hours of their arrival, the Jews had been stripped of their possessions and valuables, gassed to death, and their bodies burned in specially designed crematoriums. Approximately 3.5 million Jews were murdered in these death camps.

Many healthy, young, and strong Jews, however, were not killed immediately. The Germans' war effort and the "Final Solution" required a great deal of manpower, so the Germans reserved large pools of Jews from the ovens for slave labor. These people, imprisoned in concentration and labor camps, were forced to work in German munitions and other factories, such as I.G. Farben and Krupps, and wherever the Nazis needed laborers. They were worked from dawn until dark without adequate food and shelter. Thousands perished, literally worked to death by the Germans and their collaborators.

In the last months of Hitler's Reich, as the German armies retreated, the Nazis began marching the prisoners still alive in the concentration camps to the territory they still controlled. The Germans forced the starving and sick Jews to walk hundreds of miles. Most died or were shot along the way. About a quarter of a million Jews died as a result of the death marches.

Jewish Resistance

The Germans' overwhelming repression and the presence of many collaborators in the various local populations severely limited the ability of the Jews to resist. Jewish resistance did occur, however, and took several forms. Staying alive, clean, and observing Jewish religious traditions constituted resistance under the dehumanizing conditions imposed by the Nazis. Other forms of resistance involved escape attempts from the ghettos and camps. Many who succeeded in escaping the ghettos lived in the forests and mountains in family camps and in fighting partisan units. Once free, though, the Jews had to contend with local residents and partisan groups who were often openly hostile. Jews also staged armed revolts in the ghettos of Vilna, Bialystok, Bedzin-Sosnowiec, Cracow, and Warsaw.

The Warsaw Ghetto Uprising was the largest ghetto revolt. Massive deportations had been held in the ghetto from July to September 1942, emptying the ghetto of the majority of Jews imprisoned there. When the Germans entered the ghetto again in January 1943 to remove several thousand more, small unorganized groups of Jews attacked them. After four days, the Germans withdrew from the ghetto, having deported far fewer people than they had intended. The Nazis reentered the ghetto on April 19, 1943, the eve of Passover, to evacuate the remaining Jews and close the ghetto. The Jews, using homemade bombs and stolen or bartered weapons, resisted and withstood the Germans for 27 days. They fought from bunkers and the sewers and evaded capture until finally the Germans burned the ghetto building by building. By May 16 the ghetto was in ruins and the uprising crushed. . . .

Righteous Gentiles

Some non-Jews resisted the Germans by hiding Jews or helping them to escape the Nazi net. These people, who often risked their lives and the lives of their families and friends to save Jews, are called Righteous Gentiles. The people of Denmark as a whole defied Hitler's orders and Germany's might by refusing to hand over their fellow Jewish citizens for slaughter. The Danes succeeded in hiding nearly 7,200 Jews and clandestinely transporting them to safety in neutral Sweden. Raoul Wallenberg, a young Swedish diplomat, saved 100,000 Hungarian Jews by issuing them passports that protected them from deportation. Oscar Schindler, a German factory owner, saved his Jewish slave laborers by singlehandedly retrieving them from transports to the concentration camps. He fed and housed them in his own labor camp and kept them working in his factory until the war was over. Some of the righteous gentiles took in Jewish children and raised them as their own, thus saving their lives.

THE HOLOCAUST'S NON-JEWISH VICTIMS

Terese Pencak Schwartz

During World World II, German leader Adolf Hitler and the Nazis committed unparalleled acts of ethnic violence collectively referred to as the Holocaust. In the following selection, Terese Pencak Schwartz writes that although most people associate the term "Holocaust victim" with Jews, in actuality five million of the eleven million victims of the Holocaust were not Jewish. Three of the five million non-Jews were Poles, she explains—victims of Hitler's goal to obliterate all traces of Polish history and culture. Schwartz describes how during the war both the Nazis and the Soviets mercilessly victimized the Polish people—Gentile and Jew alike. Schwartz currently is researching non-Jewish Holocaust survivors and rescuers.

Growing up in a Polish community, and raised by parents who survived the Holocaust, I heard many stories about the atrocities of this World War II horror. I learned how one of my family's homes in Poland was burned to the ground by Nazis. I learned that my uncle was shot in the head by Nazi soldiers because the family was hiding a Jewish woman. Painful as it was for them to speak about it, my parents felt it was important that I knew the stories of the Holocaust.

It was only after I moved to the Los Angeles area several years ago that I realized that many people were not aware that millions of victims of the Holocaust were *not* Jewish. Outside the Polish community, I heard very little mention about the five million non-Jewish victims—usually referred to as "the others."

Whenever I would say that my parents were survivors of the Holocaust, people would look at me oddly and say, "Oh, I didn't know you were Jewish?" I realized that most people were not aware of any other Holocaust victims except Jews. This concerned me.

I am Jewish. I converted in 1978 after studying at the University of Judaism one year before marrying a Jewish man. I belong to a temple where my daughter attends religious school. I love the Jewish religion and I admire the Jewish community. In no way do I want to diminish

Reprinted, with permission, from "Five Million Forgotten," by Terese Pencak Schwartz, The Holocaust Forgotten Memorial, 1997, published at www.holocaustforgotten.com.

the enormous magnitude of the victimization and murder of the 5,860,000 Jewish people during the Holocaust. The Jews were singled out by the Nazis for total extermination—a significant fact that I do not repudiate, nor want to diminish in any way. The Jewish people have done an extraordinary job of making the younger generation around the world aware of their persecution and the immense tragedy of the Holocaust.

Non-Jewish Holocaust Victims

But what about "the others"? There were five million of them. Who were they? Whose children, whose mothers and fathers were they? How could five million human beings have been killed and forgotten? I began my research. After studying several carefully-documented books, and interviewing non-Jewish survivors, I found more information about the five million forgotten than I had ever imagined—information that most people are not aware of. Polish people suffered enormously during the Holocaust—Jews and non-Jews.

Eleven million precious lives were lost during the Holocaust of World War II. Six million of these were Polish citizens. Half of these Polish citizens were non-Jews. On August 22, 1939, a few days before the official start of World War II, Adolf Hitler authorized his commanders, with these infamous words, to kill "without pity or mercy, all men, women, and children of Polish descent or language. Only in this way can we obtain the living space [lebensraum] we need."

Heinrich Himmler echoed Hitler's decree: "All Poles will disappear from the world. . . . It is essential that the great German people should consider it as its major task to destroy all Poles."

On September 1, 1939, Hitler invaded Poland from three directions. Hitler's invincible troops attacked from the west, the north and the south. Poland never had a chance. By October 8, 1939, Polish Jews and non-Jews were stripped of all rights and were subject to special legislation. Rationing, which allowed for only bare sustenance of food and medicine, was quickly set up. Young Polish men were forcibly drafted into the German army. The Polish language was forbidden. Only the German language allowed. All secondary schools and colleges were closed. The Polish press was liquidated. Libraries and bookshops were burned. Polish art and culture were destroyed. Polish churches and religious buildings were burned. Most of the priests were arrested and sent to concentration camps. Street signs were either destroyed or changed to new German names. Polish cities and towns were renamed in German. It was Hitler's goal to obliterate all traces of Polish history and culture.

Hundreds of Polish community leaders, mayors, local officials, priests, teachers, lawyers, judges, senators, doctors were executed in public. Much of the rest of the so-called *Intelligentsia*, the Polish leading class, was sent to concentration camps where they later died.

A Reign of Terror

The first mass execution of World War II took place in Wawer, a town near Warsaw, Poland, on December 27, 1939, when 107 Polish non-Jewish men were taken from their homes in the middle of the night and shot. This was just the beginning of the street roundups and mass executions that continued throughout the war. The goal of these executions, deportations, and the ruthless domination of citizens was to terrorize all Poles into docile subservience.

At the same time, on the eastern border of Poland, the Soviet Union invaded and quickly conquered. Germany and the Soviet Union divided Poland in half. The western half, occupied by the Nazis, became a new German territory: "General Gouvernment." The eastern half was incorporated within the adjoining Russian border by Soviet "elections." This new border "realignment" conferred Soviet citizenship on its new Polish inhabitants. And all young Polish men were subject to being drafted into the Soviet army.

Just like the Nazis, the Soviets also reigned terror in Poland. The Soviets took over Polish businesses, Polish factories and destroyed churches and religious buildings. The Polish currency (zloty) was removed from circulation. All Polish banks were closed and savings accounts were blocked.

During the war, Poland lost 45% of her doctors, 57% of her attorneys, 40% of her professors, 30% of her technicians, more than 18% of her clergy, and most of her journalists. Poland's educated class was purposely targeted because the Nazis knew that this would make it easier to control the country.

Death and Destruction

Non-Jews of Polish descent suffered over 100,000 deaths at Auschwitz. The Germans forcibly deported approximately 2,000,000 Polish Gentiles into slave labor for the Third Reich. The Russians deported almost 1,700,000 Polish non-Jews to Siberia. Men, women and children were forced from their homes with no warning. Transferred in cattle cars in freezing weather, many died on the way. Polish children who possessed Aryan-looking characteristics were wrenched from their mother's arms and placed in German homes to be raised as Germans.

The Polish people were classified by the Nazis according to their racial characteristics. The ones who appeared Aryan were deported to Lodz for further racial examination. Most of the others were sent to the Reich to work in slave labor camps. The rest were sent to Auschwitz to die. Polish Christians and Catholics were actually the first victims of the notorious German death camp. For the first 21 months after it began in 1940, Auschwitz was inhabited almost exclusively by Polish non-Jews. The first ethnic Pole died in June 1940 and the first Jew died in October 1942.

Because of the obliteration of the Polish press by the Nazis, most of the world was not aware, including many parts of Nazi-occupied Poland, of the atrocities going on. Even to this day, much documentation of the Holocaust is not available. The entire records of Auschwitz were stolen by the Soviets and not returned. It was Hitler's goal to rewrite history. The Nazis destroyed books, monuments, historical inscriptions. They began a forceful campaign of propaganda to convince the world of their invincible superiority and power and likewise the inferiority and weakness of the Polish people.

While there is no argument that Hitler abhorred the Jews and caused almost six million to be ruthlessly killed, often non-Jewish victims are tragically forgotten from Holocaust remembrances. Eleven million precious human lives were lost during the Holocaust. Five million of these were non-Jewish. Three million were Polish Christians and Catholics. It would be very sad to forget even one precious life extinguished so ruthlessly. It would be a tragedy to forget five million.

THE ARAB-ISRAELI CONFLICT

J.J. Goldberg

In the following selection, J.J. Goldberg explores the history leading up to the ethnic violence that has marked Arab-Israeli relations
for more than half a century. He attributes the dispute between
the Jews and the Palestinian Arabs to their competing claims to
the land of Israel, formerly known as Palestine. The catalyst for the
present conflict, says Goldberg, was the creation of the Jewish
State of Israel and the rapidly growing number of foreign Jews who
settled there, pushing out the Arab inhabitants. He relates how the
violence and the killings escalated over time, fueled by festering
mistrust and misunderstanding on both sides. Goldberg is the
author of *Jewish Power: Inside the American Jewish Establishment.*

The conflict between Arabs and Israelis has been one of the longest
and most complex of the twentieth century. It has led to four wars,
thousands of deaths, and the deep involvement of the United States,
the Soviet Union, and other nations. But at its heart, the dispute is
rooted in the strong and ancient claims of two peoples—Jews and
Palestinians—to a single tiny piece of land in the heart of the Middle
East. The following primer is designed to answer basic questions
about the Arab-Israeli conflict. How did it start? Why has it lasted so
long? And what are the chances for peace?

The Core of the Conflict

What are the roots of the conflict?

At the center of the conflict are the powerful competing claims of
both Jews and Palestinian Arabs to the land known as Israel—a conflict that dates back thousands of years.

Jewish claims originate in Biblical times, when a Jewish kingdom—
centered in Jerusalem and ruled by kings, among them David and
Solomon—dominated the area. But by 70 A.D., the Romans had conquered the Jewish nation and forced its people off the land. The Jews
called their period of wandering without a homeland the Diaspora,
from the Greek word for dispersed. Although they settled in countries
the world over, for centuries afterward Jews prayed that one day their
people would return to Israel.

Meanwhile, Israel—which the Romans called Palestine—came under Arab domination. By the ninth century, the majority of the population were Muslims—followers of the Islamic prophet Mohammed—who, like the Jews, considered Jerusalem one of their holiest cities. For the next 10 centuries Palestine would be under Islamic rule.

In the late nineteenth century, Jews in Europe—who suffered from horrendous persecution—began to organize efforts to create a homeland in Israel. They called their movement Zionism—after the Hebrew word for Jerusalem. By 1910, 25,000 Jews had moved to Palestine. At first, the local Palestine Arab population lived in peace with the new Jewish settlers. But as the number of Jewish settlers grew, Palestinian anger and nationalism began to grow. The two groups frequently clashed. The stage was set for an enduring conflict.

The Creation of Israel

How was the modern state of Israel created?

In November 1917, the British captured Palestine from Turkey, which had ruled it since 1517. In 1922, the League of Nations (predecessor of the United Nations) granted Britain a "mandate" to govern Palestine and to help Zionist settlers build a Jewish national home there.

In that same year, Britain cut off the eastern half of Palestine and created a separate country, at first called Transjordan ("Across-the-Jordan"), and later Jordan. It was ruled by an Arab nobleman from the Arabian Peninsula, Abdullah, the grandfather of King Hussein, Jordan's present-day ruler. Britain ruled the rest of Palestine for 25 years, until hostilities between Jewish settlers and Arabs grew too fierce to handle. In 1947, the British handed the matter over to the United Nations (UN).

Meanwhile, thousands of Jews who had survived the "Holocaust"—Nazi Germany's extermination of European Jews during World War II—sought out Palestine as a refuge. As a result, world support for the creation of a Jewish homeland increased dramatically. Finally, in November 1947, the UN voted to "partition" Palestine into two states, one Jewish and one Palestinian Arab. Middle Eastern Arab states quickly rejected the plan, however, insisting Palestine should become a single Arab country.

Arab vs. Israeli

Who started the present conflict, the Israelis or the Arabs?

Most Arabs argue that the establishment of Israel created the conflict by bringing foreign settlers into Palestine and dispossessing the original inhabitants. Most Israelis believe the Arabs started the conflict by refusing to accept the creation of Israel and trying to destroy it.

On May 15, 1948, the day Israel declared its independence, the armies of five Arab states invaded it. After a year of war, Israel held more territory than it had been given by the UN in the first place. The defeated Arab states signed cease-fire agreements, but they refused to sign a peace treaty, claiming that a state of war continued to exist.

As for the Arab state of Palestine set up by the UN, those parts of it not taken by Israel were absorbed into Egypt and Jordan. Palestinian Arabs have called the war the "Catastrophe." One million Palestinians, left without farms or homes, fled Israel in its aftermath. Yet most of them were turned away from other Arab nations and wound up in UN-run refugee camps.

What are the "Occupied Territories"?

In June 1967, Egypt and Syria suddenly mobilized their armies on Israel's borders. Fearing an attack, Israel launched a surprise attack of its own. The next day, King Hussein of Jordan joined the war to help his fellow Arabs.

Over the next six days, Israel defeated all three armies and captured large stretches of their land. From Egypt, Israel won the Sinai and the Gaza strip. From Syria, it captured the Golan Heights, a plateau overlooking Israel's northern valleys. From Jordan, Israel took the West Bank, a hilly region of farming villages that formed the heart of ancient Israel and was to have been the center of the Palestinian state in 1948.

After the war, Israel announced that all the territories except East Jerusalem would be returned as part of an overall peace agreement. The Arabs, however, refused to negotiate. That November, the UN passed Security Council Resolution 242. It called on Israel to withdraw from the occupied territories in return for "secure and recognized boundaries." This, too, was rejected by the Arabs.

In winning the West Bank, Israel acquired most of historic Israel, including such emotionally charged places as Bethlehem and Hebron. Most important, it gained the Old City of Jerusalem and the Western Wall, the last remnant of the Temple of Solomon and Judaism's holiest shrine.

The Palestinians

Who speaks for the Palestinians?

When Israel was created, about 185,000 Palestinians stayed on as citizens of the new state. They live in their own villages and are represented in Israel's parliament by their own political parties. Today, Israeli Arabs number about 750,000, one-sixth of Israel's 4.9 million population. The majority of Palestinians, nearly 1.7 million, live in the occupied territories. Nearly 1 million Palestinians also live in Jordan, while perhaps another 700,000 are scattered around the world.

In 1964, the Palestine Liberation Organization (PLO) was formed in Jordan. The organization called for the destruction of Israel, the expulsion of most of its Jews, and the creation of an Arab state. Under the leadership of its chairman, Yasir Arafat, the PLO steadily gained stature as the "sole legitimate representative" of the Palestinian people. It opened "embassies" and even won observer status at the United Nations.

Nevertheless, the PLO alienated many in the West by engaging in acts of terror and assassinating Palestinians who did not accept its supremacy. Over the years, the PLO has tried to improve its image by moderating its tactics and positions. In 1988, the PLO declared that it would accept Israel's right to exist and renounced the use of terrorism. But because the PLO refuses to include these changes in its charter—or constitution—Israel refuses to deal with it.

The PLO's prestige was seriously damaged as a result of its support for Iraq during the Gulf War. That position angered most Arab states as well as the West.

What is the Palestinian uprising or "intifada"?

In Arabic, intifada means "a shaking off." For a generation of young Palestinians, who have lived their entire lives under Israeli military rule, the word means "shaking off" of Israeli occupation of the West Bank and Gaza Strip.

The intifada began in December 1987. The primary causes were Palestinian frustration with living conditions in the occupied territories and lack of progress toward ending the occupation. The uprising was sparked by an auto accident in the Gaza Strip in which a Palestinian was killed by an Israeli driver. Rumors quickly spread that the killing was revenge for the stabbing death of an Israeli in a Gaza market a day earlier. The rumor led to rioting, the rioting spread, and before anyone realized what was happening, the intifada was born.

Since then, some 1,000 Palestinians and 55 Israelis have been killed and more than 40,000 Palestinians have been arrested. Israel's harsh handling of the uprising has caused dissent at home and drawn sharp criticism from abroad. But the Israeli government insists that tough measures are needed to preserve security in the territories.

Obstacles to Peace

Is there any chance for peace?

There is a chance, but it will not be easy. Mistrust, misunderstanding, and hatred are deeply noted on both sides. In many ways, the obstacles to peace are the same as they were four decades ago. On the one hand, Arab states need to come to terms with the Jewish state in their midst. On the other hand, Israel must recognize the aspirations of Palestinians for a homeland of their own.

RACIAL VIOLENCE IN THE UNITED STATES IN THE 1960s

William Manchester

In the following selection, William Manchester paints a vivid picture of the racial tensions and violence that spread across the United States in the 1960s. He relates how a nonviolent civil rights march to Selma, Alabama, ended in three racist murders that helped convince young black activists to reject the nonviolence philosophy of Martin Luther King Jr. Manchester also chronicles the race riot that erupted in 1965 in Watts, a poor and predominantly black inner-city district of Los Angeles, when a white patrolman stopped a young African American on suspicion of drunk driving. Watts, explains Manchester, was only the beginning of violent clashes between whites and blacks during the 1960s. Manchester is a former correspondent for the *Baltimore Sun* and the author of numerous works of nonfiction, including *The Glory and the Dream: A Narrative History of America*, from which the following selection is excerpted. He also taught at Wesleyan University in Middletown, Connecticut, for many years.

In appealing to a joint session of Congress for the voting Rights Act of 1965, U.S. President Lyndon Johnson concluded his speech with a phrase which had become hallowed by the blood and tears of a new generation of black Americans marching for justice. He said that their cause "must be our cause too. Because it's not just Negroes, but really it's all of us who must overcome the crippling legacy of bigotry and injustice. *And we shall overcome.*"

That was fine liberal eloquence, but at times it appeared to be a doubtful prediction. The eleventh anniversary of the Supreme Court's ruling in Brown v. Board of Education passed on May 17, and racism seemed stronger than ever. C. Vann Woodward, Sterling Professor of History at Yale, said, "Negroes now have less contact with whites in schools than they did a generation ago." Between the middle of 1964 and the middle of 1965 the Ku Klux Klan made its greatest membership gains ever, including the Reconstruction era. . . .

Black Sunday: Violence in Selma

C. Vann Woodward wrote in 1965 that "insofar as federal laws are capable of coping" with segregation and prejudice, "Congress has just about fulfilled its role." The capstone of such legislation was the voting act of that year. In January Martin Luther King called a press conference to point out that three million of the five million blacks in the South old enough to vote were not registered, and to announce that he was launching an all-out registration drive. It would open in Selma, Alabama, where 325 of 15,000 potential black voters were registered, as against 9,300 of 14,000 whites. Typically, Dr. King led the first group of Negroes ever to stay at Selma's Hotel Albert, previously all-white, and typically he was punched and kicked by a white segregationist while signing the hotel register. His assailant was fined one hundred dollars and sentenced to sixty days in jail, which King thought was a good start toward respect for the law, but then the drive stalled. The blunt truth was that most of Selma's Negroes were indifferent to the right to vote. Something dramatic was needed to arouse them. It was provided—again, this was characteristic—by rural whites who murdered a black would-be voter in nearby Perry County. Local civil rights leaders counted on that, on Sheriff Jim Clark's short temper, and on Governor George Wallace's showboating to revive their campaign.

They declared that on March 7 they would stage a protest march. Negro and white sympathizers would hike from Selma to Montgomery, fifty-four miles away, moving straight down the middle of route 80, the Jefferson Davis Highway. Wallace promptly banned the demonstration as a menace to commerce and public safety and sent a hundred state troopers to reinforce Sheriff Clark, who gave a sign of his allegiance to the past by rounding up a mounted posse. On March 7—which would enter Alabama history and folklore as "Black Sunday"—six hundred Negroes and a few white partisans of their cause defiantly marched from the Brown's Chapel African Methodist Episcopal Church to the Edmund Pettus Bridge, spanning the Alabama River. There they ran into Clark's horsemen and troopers wearing gas masks. When they ignored a two-minute warning to disperse, possemen waded into them swinging billy clubs and wet bullwhips. Yellow clouds of tear gas belched from the ranks of the troopers. Routed, the blacks stumbled and crawled back to the church. Accompanying them were television cameramen, whose footage guaranteed that Selma would become overnight a symbol of oppression.

Dr. King had been preaching in Atlanta on Black Sunday. Dropping everything, he flew to Selma, announced that he would lead a second march on Tuesday, and called on clergymen of both races to join him. Over three hundred white ministers, priests, and rabbis responded. . . .

King was turned around that same evening by the first of three murders arising from the Selma crisis, all of whites who sympathized with the civil rights movement. The Reverend James J. Reeb, a Boston Unitarian, was set upon by red-neck hoodlums as he left a Negro restaurant and was beaten to death. . . .

Innocent Victims

Leaving Selma on March 21 there had been 3,200 in the procession; arriving in Montgomery four days later there were 25,000. Dr. King spoke to them on the grounds of the statehouse, which a century ago had been the capital of the Confederacy. He ended by crying four times, "Glory hallelujah!" They disbanded and heavy traffic carried them back on route 80 to Selma. A sullen clump of Ku Klux Klansmen watched them go. As the stream of cars thinned Klansmen moved in for the second murder.

The victim was Viola Gregg Liuzzo, a red-haired Detroit housewife and the mother of five. . . . A car full of Klansmen drew alongside [her car] on a lonely stretch of road. One of the white hoodlums, an auto mechanic, fired a 38-caliber pistol at her head. She collapsed with blood spurting from her temple; the car careened into a ditch. . . .

The third killing was of an Episcopalian seminarian from New Hampshire who was gunned down in a grocery. The killer, a part-time deputy sheriff, pleaded self-defense and was found innocent by a jury of twelve white Alabama men. . . .

Selma inspired the voting rights act—Johnson said as much in asking Congress for it on March 15—and the country credited it to Dr. King. It proved to be the peak of his reputation. The events of the previous year in Mississippi having created the first serious doubts about nonviolence, the Alabama murders confirmed the suspicions of the new generation of black activists. These skeptics left Selma convinced that King had nothing more to teach them. The vast majority of the Negro people disagreed. . . . The majority yearned for peace—a majority has always wanted it—but the country was entering a new period, and one of its most striking qualities would be an affinity for violence. . . . A gear had shifted somewhere in the universe. Search and destroy, emerging in Vietnam during the same months in 1965, was one expression of the emerging mood, the Selma murders were another; still others would crowd upon one another in the succeeding months and years as Negro rage and frustration which had been repressed for a century now erupted.

Building Tensions

The new inner city temper emerged in Los Angeles on Wednesday, August 11, 1965, in a shabby Negro district [called Watts] of low-faded stucco houses, suggestive of certain poor areas in Puerto Rico, which lay under the approaches to Los Angeles International Airport. Trash never seemed to be properly collected there. There was litter everywhere—broken glass, rusty cans, rotting chicken bones, empty Tokay bottles—and the quality of life was further diminished by the typical white policeman, also known locally as The Man, who had a way of stopping black citizens and demanding, "Let's see your I.D."

That August evening Lee Minikus, an officer of the California Highway Patrol, wanted a look at the I.D. of a young Negro named Marquette Frye; he intended to take him in on suspicion of drunken driving. A knot of people, gathering around, kidded both Minikus and his suspect. It all seemed low-key and harmless, but beneath the surface tension was building. Los Angeles was in the fourth day of a brutal heat wave. People were outdoors, ready to assemble quickly at the promise of excitement. The arrest was taking place at the corner of Avalon Boulevard and Imperial Highway, a busy L.A. intersection through which passed a constant stream of white drivers, often behind the wheels of expensive cars. Most inauspicious of all was the neighborhood. It was 98 percent black, with a population density of 27.3 people per acre (the figure was 7.4 for Los Angeles County as a whole). Negro immigrants had been arriving here in massive numbers since the early 1940s, when an average of 2,000 each month came to work in war industries. Now 420,000 of the 2,731,000 inhabitants of the city were black. Yet in this ghetto there were just five blacks on the 205-man police force. And every month in 1965 another 1,000 Negroes poured into these swarming warrens, often looking for jobs that no longer existed. . . .

Racial Rioting in Watts

At 7:45 P.M. that Wednesday, California Highway Patrolman Minikus took the Frye youth into custody. Almost immediately he was in trouble. Among those attracted by the winking red light of his squad car was the prisoner's mother. At first she rebuked her son. Then she turned on the police officer. As her manner became distraught and the murmurs of the spectators less good-humored, Minikus nervously radioed for reinforcements. Then he made two mistakes. He attempted to force Frye into the squad car and he turned his back on Frye's mother. She jumped on it. As other officers arrived they pried her loose, and when the crowd began to mutter indignantly they held it at bay with shotguns. Minikus got away with his man, but the price had been exorbitant. Already the use of force was beginning to inspire distorted accounts of what had happened, and with each passing hour the stories grew taller. . . . Aroused, the crowd pelted policemen with stones and bottles. By 10 P.M. the spectators had been transformed into a mob which set upon passersby, overturned cars, and smashed shop display windows. The familiar stages of riot escalation now appeared. Police sealed off eight blocks at 11 P.M. Two hours later the rioters burst free and roved Watts, two thousand strong, waylaying strangers, breaking everything fragile, and looting the stores.

At 3 A.M. the level of violence fell—rioters must sleep, too—and police patrols imposed a semblance of order in the ghetto. In the morning shop managers called their insurance companies, clerks cleaned up the mess, and those who knew nothing about riots assumed this one was over. Their disillusionment began at 7:45 P.M. that Thursday, just twenty-four hours after the arrest of young Frye. At first it was all a repetition of Wednesday evening: youths pouncing on passing autos, pelting cops with bricks, breaking windows. The change came at 4 A.M. At that hour the day before, a peace of exhaustion had fallen over the ghetto. This time a second shift of rioters spilled into the streets. These men were older and more vicious. They were also armed. . . . The ghetto violence was approaching the force of an insurrection, but the authorities didn't realize it yet. . . .

The truth was revealed to them at 10 A.M., when two white salesmen were attacked in the first incident of daytime violence. At 11 A.M. a policeman wounded a black looter. Governor Edmund Brown, on vacation in Greece, read reports of the growing disorders and hurried home; his lieutenant governor granted a request from the L.A. police chief for National Guard troops. The first contingent of Guardsmen reached Watts Friday afternoon. Even as they were being briefed in an elementary school the version they heard was being outdated by new developments in the ghetto. More than 5,000 rioters now roamed a 150-block area, firing buildings with Molotov cocktails and ambushing firemen who answered the alarms. Watts claimed its first fatality, a sheriff's deputy mortally wounded in the stomach, at 9:40 P.M. Three other deaths quickly followed. National Guard soldiers entering the district with fixed bayonets saw looters, their way illumined by major fires, carrying guns, appliances, liquor, jewelry—everything of value— from the shops of the ghetto. Crudely lettered signs outside some stores read "Black Brother," "Soul Brother," "Negro Owned," and "Owned by a Brother." Some had been robbed anyway. . . .

On Saturday snipers on rooftops began picking off soldiers and policemen. Firemen were issued bulletproof vests. The Guard force grew to 10,000 men, then to 14,000; a curfew was imposed on 40 square miles Saturday and on 46 square miles Sunday. Intermittent shoot-outs continued until the early hours of Wednesday, August 18, when officers seized 35 blacks after a gunfight at a Black Muslim mosque. That was the end of it. During the six days of madness 34 had been killed, 898 hurt, and over 4,000 arrested. Losses were put at 45 million dollars.

The Watts devastation was called the worst race riot since Detroit in 1943, but it was really in a class by itself. While the death toll was the same, the damage in Detroit had been less than a million dollars. There was trouble elsewhere, too. Coincident with Watts, the West Side of Chicago ran amok when a fire truck, answering an alarm in West Garfield Park on August 12, struck and killed a black woman. Negroes fought cops and 2,000 Guardsmen for two nights, looting and hurling bottles at whites. Over 100 were arrested and 67 hurt. And in Springfield, Massachusetts, far from the ghettos of the great cities, the arrest of eighteen blacks outside a nightclub gave rise to accusations of brutality against seven cops; Molotov cocktail bombings of stores owned by whites then led to mass arrests and, once more, the calling of the National Guard. A protest march by 4,000 Springfield Negroes ended at City Hall, where George Wiley, assistant director of the Congress of Racial Equality (CORE), told them that "the civil rights struggle in the North" would be "longer, bloodier, and more bitter" than it had been in the South. . . .

1966: A Year of Rebellion

If the summer of racial disorders had been hot in 1965, it had also been short. Until Watts burst into flame that second week in August there had been hope that the country might make it that year without a major riot. The next year was a different story. Again Los Angeles sounded the tocsin, but this time it was in March that a gang of Negro students stoned the auto of a white teacher there, attacked other whites, and turned to looting. Angeleno policemen had learned a lot the year before; this new threat was suppressed overnight with only two deaths. Yet if L.A. escaped with fewer scars, the rest of the nation did not. It almost seemed as though every large black community in the United States was in rebellion against society. In Washington, D.C., Negroes rose in April. By May three California cities were embattled. Cleveland erupted in late June, and Omaha, Des Moines, and Chicago two weeks after that. Next came Cleveland, and then in swift succession Brooklyn, Baltimore, Perth Amboy, Providence, Minneapolis, Milwaukee, Detroit, Dayton, Atlanta, San Francisco, and St. Louis; Pompano Beach, Florida; Cordele, Georgia; Cicero, Illinois; and Lansing, Muskegon, Benton Harbor, and Jackson, Michigan. By the end of the summer the toll was seven dead, over 400 hurt, some 3,000 arrested, and more than five million dollars lost to vandals, looters, and arsonists. By the end of 1966, America had been scarred by forty-three race riots that year. . . .

On June 5 James H. Meredith announced that he was leaving Memphis to hike 225 miles to Mississippi's state capitol in Jackson. His motive was to prove that American Negroes were unafraid. . . . Guided by a feeling of "divine responsibility," as he had called it in *Three Years in Mississippi*, . . . he believed that destiny awaited him in his native state, and he was correct, destiny in this case represented by a middle-aged, unemployed white Mississippian named Aubrey James Norvell. At 4:15 P.M. on the second day of the journey, Meredith and a convoy of FBI agents were striding along U.S. 51 just south of Hernando, Mississippi, when Norvell rose out of the bushes beside the road. "James Meredith!" he yelled. "James Meredith! I only want Meredith!" He fired three shotgun blasts. Doctors in a Memphis hospital found Meredith peppered with birdshot.

None of the wounds was serious. Norvell's real damage had been done to the notion that Meredith's walk needn't be taken seriously. The burst of gunfire had turned it into a crusade, and everyone in the movement wanted to be part of it. . . .

The day after Norvell's ambush [Stokely] Carmichael [chairman of SNCC] told a Memphis rally, "The Negro is going to take what he deserves from the white man." King deplored such demagoguery; Roy Whitney of the National Association for the Advancement of Colored People (NAACP) and Whitney M. Young Jr. of the Urban League agreed. But the rhetoric of the young militants became more bellicose. In Philadelphia, Mississippi, where in the freedom Summer of 1964 death had come to three members of the movement—two of them white—a white Mississippian was wounded by gunfire in the dark, and Ralph Featherstone of SNCC, far from regretting the incident, exulted that blacks were no longer meek, that "their reaction is shot for shot." Carmichael spoke up for the Black Panther political party. In Yazoo City young Negroes chanted, "Hey! Hey! Whattaya know! White folks must go—must go!" and that night at the Yazoo City fairgrounds Willie Ricks, a twenty-three-year-old member of SNCC known as "the Reverend" because of his evangelical style, mounted a flatbed truck and delivered a sermon of hate that made older Negro leaders shudder. He spoke of the blood of whites flowing and repeatedly described his goal in two explosive words: "Black power!"

In Greenwood, forty-five miles away, Carmichael was emerging from seven hours in jail. . . . [He] had been arrested while trying to erect tents on a Negro school playground. He heard about Ricks's speech just as he himself was climbing another flatbed truck to address a Greenwood rally. Using the repetition and question-and-response techniques which civil rights leaders had adopted so successfully from Negro preachers, he reminded his audience that he had been apprehended by police in a Negro schoolyard. "Everybody owns our neighborhoods except us. . . . Now we're going to get something and we're going to get some representing. We ain't going to worry about whether it's white—maybe black. Don't be ashamed. We . . . want . . . black . . . power!"

They shouted, "That's right!" and he took up the theme: "We . . . want . . . black power! We . . . want . . . black . . . power! . . .

What did it mean? Roy Wilkins had no doubts: "The term 'black power' means anti-white power . . . It has to mean going it alone. It has to mean separatism. We of the NAACP will have none of this." Wilkins called the phrase "the father of hatred and the mother of violence." Martin Luther King said much the same thing at first, though later, seeing that the coalition of civil rights groups was coming apart over the issue, he hedged, interpreting it as "an appeal to racial pride, an appeal to the Negro not to be ashamed of being black, and the transfer of the powerlessness of the Negro into positive, constructive power." McKissick saw it as an appeal to joint action: "Unless we can get around to unifying black power, we're going to be in bad shape." But Charles Evers, brother of the martyred Medgar Evers and the ranking NAACP worker in Mississippi, warned that "If we are marching these roads for black supremacy, we are doomed," and A. Philip Randolph [head of the Brotherhood of Sleeping Car Porters], deploring the war cry as "a menace to racial peace and prosperity," said that "No Negro who is fighting for civil rights can support black power, which is opposed to civil rights and integration."

A nationwide *New York Times* survey reported that the dissension among civil rights leaders in Mississippi was reducing public support for the movement. An opinion poll found that 77 percent of whites felt the black power creed was hurting the black cause. . . .

A Break in Leadership

An open break between the old leaders and the new was inevitable. It came at Canton, near the end of the Meredith March, on June 23, after police had refused to let them pitch their tents on another school playground. Refusing to disperse, twenty-five hundred blacks stood their ground. Carmichael cried, "The time for running has come to an end." It hadn't really—when the police charged with nightsticks and tear gas the people scattered—but when King turned down a proposal that they try to put up the tents anyway, the SNCC leadership deserted him. . . .

Philip Randolph, appalled by the violent confrontations between slum blacks and policemen, suggested in September that "the time has come when the street marches and demonstrations have about run their course." He proposed a new approach, "a shift from the streets to the conference table." In October he, Wilkins, Young, Rustin, and three other veterans of the civil rights struggle signed a statement repudiating violence, rioting,and demagoguery, and concluding: "We not only welcome, we urge the full cooperation of white Americans.". . .

Declaring War

For a time Carmichael took a conciliatory line. . . . It didn't last. . . . Carmichael was replaced as SNCC's chairman by an even more violent racist, H. Rap Brown. When much of downtown Cincinnati went up in flames during five terrible days and nights of Molotov cocktails, Brown told reporters that there would be no peace "until the honky cops get out." Then he said: "SNCC has declared war."

CHAPTER 3

ETHNIC VIOLENCE IN THE UNITED STATES

Contemporary Issues
Companion

HATE CRIMES: A GROWING THREAT

Gordon Witkin and Jeannye Thornton

In the following selection, Gordon Witkin and Jeannye Thornton focus on the growing incidence of racist hate crimes across the United States. According to the authors, "in-your-face racism is bubbling to the surface again." The majority of racial hate crimes, they say, are committed by white males in their teens or early twenties. The authors point out these young men are often associated with or members of hate groups such as the Ku Klux Klan. Civil right experts believe that talk radio and the Internet have aided the rapid spread of bias and hate, the authors report. Witkin and Thornton both work for *U.S. News & World Report*, Witkin as a senior editor and Thornton as a reporter.

They called themselves the "Lords of Chaos." Five of them were superior students at Riverdale High School in Fort Myers, Fla., advanced in math, computers and art. The sixth—their leader, police say—was 19-year-old Kevin Foster, who was better known for his hatred of blacks than for his artistic abilities: He allegedly drew a crude cartoon depicting hooded figures standing next to a burning cross holding a crucified black man, with the words "Black BBQ" scrawled below. The Lords "didn't fit the mold of bad boys," says Riverdale principal Robert Durham. "They did all the things parents expect them to do. These could be anyone's kids."

Earlier in 1996, police say, these Everyman's kids burned an abandoned bottling plant, pulled an armed robbery and stole a car. And authorities charge that after music teacher Mark Schwebes, 32, caught the Lords planning to burn a school auditorium, they went to his house, knocked on his door and killed him with a shotgun blast in the face. After that, police claim, the Lords were planning a "Terror Night" at Disney World in Orlando. The idea was to assault some Disney characters, steal their costumes and walk around the park shooting African-Americans. Five Lords were arrested the night before that was to occur; four of them have been charged with Schwebes's murder.

The existence of groups like the Lords of Chaos and the epidemic of church fires across the South are peeling the lid off an alarming phenomenon: Despite the gains of the civil rights struggle, in-your-face racism is bubbling to the surface again. "There is in our society today, more so than 20 or 30 years ago, a greater tolerance for intolerance," says Abraham Foxman, national director of the Anti-Defamation League of B'nai B'rith.

Mainstream Racism

Statistics on hate crimes are soft, and federal data-gathering on the subject lags, so it's hard to draw broad conclusions. But the best estimates are that between 10,000 and 40,000 hate crimes are committed annually in America—about 60 percent by whites, and about 60 percent motivated by racial bias. Whites have no monopoly on hatred: Of the 5,842 hate crimes reported to the FBI for 1994, the most recent year available, 1,901 were racial incidents directed at whites—including 908 antisemitic religious incidents.

Stockton College criminal justice Prof. Brian Levin, formerly of the Southern Poverty Law Center, says 56 percent of bias-related homicides are committed by offenders under 21. Adds Prof. Jack Levin of Northeastern University: "The bad news is that this is coming from the center where most of us live. These are our children—the boy next door, the young man at the next desk—who can't handle diversity and whose rage translates into violence. Many are red-blooded, hot-dog-and-apple-pie Americans. We aren't talking about racism under a rock but in the mainstream of our culture."

There are reasons for the church fires—vandalism, insurance fraud and revenge among them. But "it's plain that racial hostility is behind many," says Assistant U.S. Attorney General Deval Patrick. Federal authorities have not uncovered any broad conspiracy, but now some almost wish they had. "The prospect of a conspiracy is a chilling thing," says Patrick. "But the prospect that these are separate acts of racism is even worse."

That may be the case. A 1993 study of some 4,000 hate crimes by Northeastern University Profs. Jack Levin and Jack McDevitt found the perpetrators were primarily white males in their teens or early 20s who seem to fall into three categories. Sixty percent are thrill seekers who don't belong to an organized group but who in an impromptu act will attack a black person or deface a church simply for the excitement, often after drinking with buddies. The second-largest category, about 35 percent, aren't members of an organized group either but see themselves as turf defenders. They might throw rocks at a new black family in the neighborhood, for instance.

Members of hate groups account for 5 percent of the perpetrators of hate crimes, but they are the most dangerous. "These folks are on a mission," says McDevitt. "They are more likely to be violent, and their violence is most likely to cause injury." A USA Today study of 14 white men investigated by the federal government for racially motivated church arsons in the 1990s found the majority to be poor, young and minimally educated. Most had been drinking on the night churches burned, but none had previous felony convictions.

Setting a Bad Example

Many hate-crime offenders also seem to be under the influence of an older leader. That might be the case for the best-known church fire suspects, Timothy Welch, 23, and Gary Cox, 22. Currently jailed in Kingstree, S.C., the pair are charged with the June 1995 torchings of the Macedonia Baptist Church in Bloomville, S.C., and the Mount Zion AME Church in nearby Greeleyville. They also are charged with beating and stabbing a retarded black man the same month. Cox and Welch had been attending local Ku Klux Klan recruiting rallies, and Welch was carrying a KKK membership card when he was arrested. Clarendon County Sheriff Hoyt Collins says Cox and Welch were "followers," not leaders. "I think they had encouragement," says Collins. "I'm not sure they had instructions."

A suit against the KKK filed on behalf of the Mount Zion Church by the Southern Poverty Law Center asserts that a speaker at one rally made "disparaging and inflammatory statements about black churches." And Cox had been living with Arthur Haley, 52, a former Klan member who also attended some rallies. Federal agents raided Haley's home in February 1996 and came away with guns and Klan paraphernalia but did not arrest him. Horace King, grand dragon of the South Carolina chapter of the Christian Knights of the Ku Klux Klan Invisible Empire, says he knew nothing of the church burnings and would have stopped them if he had. Haley declined to speak with *U.S. News*. Lawyers for Cox and Welch did not return phone calls.

The Klan and other white supremacist groups have long denounced affirmative action, welfare, immigration and race-based congressional districting, and now those issues have become mainstream political controversies. Grand Dragon King told *U.S. News* that African-Americans "hand down welfare from one generation to the next." Klan member Herbert Rowell told the *State* newspaper in Columbia, S.C., that black churches tell members how to get on the dole: "Have you ever noticed that when there's free cheese or milk and stuff? We don't know nothing about it, but they're the first in line."

Affirmative action is another target. "We've given blacks every opportunity in the form of affirmative action and quotas," said a posting on the World Wide Web from "Aryan True." "It's not opportunity they want, they want control of the country." Grand Dragon King was upset by a minority set-aside program at Columbia Metropolitan Airport. "White people have no security because of affirmative action," he said. "They can take away a job and give it to a black. The best qualified ought to get the job and that's it."

Nonwhite immigrants come in for criticism, too. "The doors should be wide open to our white brothers and sisters from every-

where in the world, and slammed shut to racial aliens," says another
recent Internet posting.

More generally, some whites fear they are being shunted aside and
are losing control. "Each race deserves its rights," says King, "but no
race should infringe upon another race's rights and push them back,
and that's what's happening today with the white race."

Talk Radio, the Internet, and Segregation

Civil rights experts think talk radio and the Internet provide new
megaphones for bias and hate. The Center for Democratic Renewal
says Darrell Flinn, the imperial wizard of the Knights of the White
Kamellia in Alabama and Louisiana, has a bimonthly cable show, *The
Klan in Akadiana,* that reaches as many as 54,000 people. Michael Har-
rison, editor and publisher of *Talkers* magazine, thinks the incidence
of racism and hatred on talk radio is exaggerated, but says 20 to 25
percent of radio talk shows occasionally air such themes. After Commerce Secretary Ron Brown's plane was reported missing, New York
talk show host Bob Grant said he feared Brown might have survived
"because at heart, I'm a pessimist." Grant was fired but was soon
picked up by another station.

Meanwhile, the struggle for racial equality and tolerance appears to
be losing out to resignation that de facto segregation is both normal
and acceptable. Greenville, S.C., high school students say that even
though their schools are integrated, blacks and whites seldom mix,
and that that's just the way it is.

In this atmosphere, stereotypes and biases can flourish. "Unfortunately, blacks are considered more lower class," says Jennie Johnson, a
17-year-old senior at Greenville's J.L. Mann High School. "In the
black community, it's not really 'cool' to be smart, so the majority
don't apply themselves academically." Gainesville, Ga., High School
held a "Farmer/Redneck Day" as part of its pre-homecoming festivi-
ties in the fall of 1995. African-American students say they were called
"nigger" all day by white classmates; school officials say the claims
may have been exaggerated.

Redneck Store

There is no lack of encouragement for this volatile mix of pride and
prejudice. South Carolina's legislature passed a law to keep the Confederate flag flying over the state house. Blacks say the flag represents
slavery; whites say it celebrates Southern heritage. In Laurens, S.C.,
John Howard has converted the old Echo Theatre into the Redneck
Shop, which is also slated to house a Ku Klux Klan museum. The
store, which opened in March 1996, sells Confederate and "redneck"
merchandise, including Ku Klux Klan pins and T-shirts with the slo-
gan, "We're here to stay."

"The goal of the shop is just to cater to people that love Confederate flags," says Howard. "And the museum is just to maintain the relics of the Klan that are part of our heritage—not to uplift it, but the history of the Klan needs to be understood. I have no intention of causing racial tension. No one's been hurt but John Howard. I've been ridiculed, persecuted and threatened."

"The Klan came into existence to oppress and inflict pain, and that store is a basic insult to what America claims it stands for," replies the Rev. David Kennedy of New Beginning Missionary Baptist Church in Laurens, who has organized several protests against the Redneck Shop. "There's going to be a fight, and our task is to make sure it's a nonviolent fight, because this town has the possibility of becoming a Little Bosnia. But if they're here to stay, so are we."

With churches still burning throughout the South, it may be hard to ensure that the fight is nonviolent.

HATE CRIMES IN AMERICA

The Leadership Conference Education Fund and the Leadership Conference on Civil Rights

The following selection is excerpted from a report on hate crimes compiled under the auspices of two Washington, D.C.–based civil rights organizations, the Leadership Conference Education Fund and the Leadership Conference on Civil Rights. According to the report, the United States has a long history of violent hate crimes against such ethnic groups as African Americans, Hispanics, Jews, Asian Americans, and Arab Americans. In recent years, the report reveals, there have been a number of disturbing acts of ethnic violence and hatred. However, federal, state, and local governments, as well as many private organizations, are increasing their efforts to combat hate crimes and other types of racial and ethnic intolerance.

Hate crimes are much more likely than other crimes to be acts of brutal violence. In comparison to other crimes, targets of hate violence are singled out because of their membership in a social group. Perpetrators are more likely to be marauding groups of predators looking for targets for their hatred. However, they can also be acquaintances, intimate partners, or family members. Because the intention is to hurt, maim, or kill, hate-motivated crimes are five times as likely as other crimes to involve assault. And these assaults are twice as likely as other assaults to cause injury and to result in hospitalization.

Thus, the individual victim of a hate crime is more likely to be severely injured in body, and in spirit as well, than the victim of an ordinary offense. Unlike someone who is robbed of a wallet, someone who is attacked for no reason except their membership in a targeted class is more likely to be beaten out of sheer cruelty. And while crime victims often ask, "Why me?" the answers are perhaps more hurtful for victims of hate crimes. Victims of hate crimes experience psychic pain regardless of the motivation of the crime. However, it is one thing to be victimized for walking down a deserted street or wearing an expensive wristwatch; but it is perhaps more painful to be victim-

Excerpted from "Cause for Concern: Hate Crimes in America," by the Leadership Conference Education Fund and Leadership Conference on Civil Rights, 1996, published at www.civilrights.org/lcef/history.html. Reprinted with permission.

ized simply for who you are. The cruelty of these crimes is magnified because they remind the victims of terrible things that had been done in the past to members of their group, or to them, their families, or their friends—pogroms against Jews, lynchings of blacks, . . . or grim memories in the minds of other groups.

As for the communities hit by hate crimes, these incidents make targeted individuals feel even more angry and alienated, increasing intergroup tensions of all kinds. Because victims are singled out because of who they are—and the targets of hate crimes are often community institutions such as synagogues or black churches—members of entire groups feel isolated and defenseless. . . . Rightly or wrongly, they often blame the police, the government, and other segments of society for their feelings of vulnerability. Sometimes, members of the groups that have been victimized lash out against members of other groups. Thus, hate crimes can set in motion a never-ending spiral of antagonism and divisiveness.

The Victims

Official statistics illuminate—but greatly understate—the scope of the problem.

As required by the 1990 law, the Federal Bureau of Investigation (FBI) releases the totals each year for the numbers of hate crimes reported by state and local law enforcement agencies around the country based on race, religion, sexual orientation or ethnicity. These national totals have fluctuated around 6,000 or more hate crimes reported each year. . . .

While more than 25,000 hate crimes reported between 1992 and 1995 are alarming enough, the FBI statistics paint only a partial portrait of the problem. In 1994, for instance, the total number of law enforcement agencies that reported hate crimes to the FBI covered only 58% of the population of the United States. In 1995, the number of reporting agencies covered 75% of the population. The findings reflect only those cases where the victims reported incidents to local law enforcement agencies and these agencies had classified these incidents as hate crimes. . . .

Yet even these incomplete statistics suggest the scope and sweep of the problem. Thus, of the 7,947 total incidents and 9,895 total offenses reported in 1995, there were 7,144 crimes against persons. . . . Sixty percent of the incidents were motivated by racial bias, 16 percent by religious bias, 13 percent by sexual-orientation bias, and 10 percent by bias against the victims' ethnicity or national origin. . . .

The Attackers

As for the perpetrators of hate crimes, a surprisingly large number may be youthful thrill-seekers, rather than hardcore haters. According to a study conducted in 1993 for Northeastern University, 60% of offenders committed crimes for the "thrill associated with the victimization." Often, the perpetrators hoped their acts of violence would gain respect from their friends—a feeling that explains why so many hate crimes are committed by gangs of young men. . . .

The second most common perpetrator of hate crimes, reported under the act, is the "reactive offender" who feels that he's answering an attack by his victim—a perceived insult, interracial dating, or the integration of his neighborhood. . . .

The least common offender, reported under the act, is the hardcore fanatic, imbued with the ideology of racial, religious, or ethnic bigotry and often a member of, or a potential recruit for, an extremist organization. While the oldest organized hate groups appear to be on the decline, new strategies are emerging where organized hatemongers incite impressionable individuals to commit acts of violence against targeted minorities.

The Hate Groups and Their Strategies

Membership in the oldest and prototypical hate groups, the various groups that bear the name "Ku Klux Klan," is near a historic low of about 5500. Another 17,000 people belong to similar groups. But these relatively low and seemingly declining numbers ought not lead people of goodwill to minimize the dangers of organized hate violence.

In part, the decline in organized hate groups is a tribute to the efforts of their opponents. For instance, in 1987 a lawsuit by the Southern Poverty Law Center resulted in a $7 million judgment against the United States Klans of America. In 1993, the Center shut down the Invisible Knights of the Ku Klux Klan, and, together with the Anti-Defamation League (ADL), successfully litigated a $12.5 million judgment against the White Aryan Resistance.

But with the success of these lawsuits, hate groups have adopted a new strategy. Instead of orchestrating and perpetrating their own acts of violence, the new hate groups increasingly are advancing their views through the Internet, literature distribution, broadcasts over public access television, and grassroots organizing. . . .

Hate groups are recruiting among two very different sectors of the population—young people alienated from society and more mainstream adults who are angry at the federal government.

Among young people, some of the readiest recruits are racist "skinheads." The "skinheads" are a cultural phenomenon dating back to the 1970's in Great Britain and the '80s here in the United States. In response to the counterculture of the '60s which favored long hair, androgynous attire, and easygoing attitudes towards life, some working class young people adopted the opposite style of grooming and clothing—shaven heads, tight-fitting jeans, and steel-toed boots. To be sure, the great majority of "skinheads" were neither violent nor racist—indeed, some espoused interracial harmony.

But some skinheads were drawn to racism and violence, attacking blacks, Jews, gays, and members of other minorities. According to the ADL, the number of racist skinheads tripled in their first five years on the American scene, and at least 37 killings can be attributed to them.

Another pool of recruits comes from the self-styled "militia" movements, paramilitary groups that are on the rise throughout the country. . . . According to the most recent ADL report, militias have operated in at least 40 states, with membership numbering at least 15,000. . . . Some of the militia organizers have been associated with racist groups, such as Aryan Nations or the Klans. And like other extremist movements, they use groups such as the militias to recruit people to their views. . . .

All in all, there are 150,000 to 200,000 hate group sympathizers, according to the Center for Democratic Renewal. And according to Klanwatch, law enforcement officials have recovered a vast array of weapons, including anti-tank and anti-aircraft weapons, military explosives, grenades, military assault rifles, Uzis, and other types of machine guns from hate groups and their sympathizers.

All this suggests that we may be witnessing not the decline of organized hate groups but their evolution. . . .

While it is reassuring that the statistics indicate relatively few people who commit hate crimes are committed members of hate groups, the predominance of less-dedicated offenders also argues for national action. . . .

The Human Face of Hate Crimes

In this most diverse society on earth, all of us are members of one or another minority—racial, religious, ethnic, cultural, national origin, sexual. That is why so many of us are vulnerable to hate crimes, and why violence motivated by bigotry has targeted so many different segments of society. . . .

Of the 7,947 hate crime incidents reported to the FBI in 1995, sixty percent—4,831—were motivated by race. Of these, 2,988 were anti-black, 1,226 were anti-white, 355 were directed against Asian-Americans or Pacific Islanders, 221 were directed against multi-racial groups, and 41 were directed against Native Americans or Alaskan Natives.

Second to racially motivated hate crimes were hate crimes motivated by religious bigotry—1,277 incidents in 1995. Of these, 1,058—approximately 82%—were directed against Jews.

The third major category of hate crimes . . . was motivated by animus against the victims' sexual orientation. . . .

The fourth category—ethnicity/national origin—accounted for 814 incidents with sixty three percent (516) directed toward Hispanics. . . .

These stories convey a sense of how hate crimes victimize Americans of different races, religions, and ethnic groups. . . .

Attacks on African-Americans

Among groups currently included in the Hate Crime Statistics Act, the greatest number of hate crimes of any kind are perpetrated against African-Americans. From the lynching to the cross-burning and the church-burning, anti-black violence has been and still remains the prototypical hate crime—an action intended not only to injure individuals but to intimidate an entire group of people. Hate crimes against African-Americans impact upon the entire society not only for the hurt they cause but for the history they recall, and perpetuate.

That is why the epidemic of fires at black churches has generated so much concern. Churches have always been the most important independent institution in the black community, and those who would attack African-Americans have often attacked their churches. . . .

An example of the historic continuity in the attacks upon black churches is the troubled history of St. John Baptist Church in Dixiana, South Carolina. Founded in 1765, the church has been the target of attacks throughout its history—a period that spans the eras of slavery, the Civil War, Reconstruction, segregation, and civil rights.

In 1983, while Sunday services were underway, a group of whites shot out the church's windows. Coming back later in the day, they scrawled "KKK" on the door, destroyed the piano, smashed the crucifix, tore up the Bibles, scattered beer cans on the pews, and even defecated on the sacrament cloth. Over the next 12 years, more than 200 people were arrested for acts of vandalism against the church. Then, on August 15, 1995, the church was burned down. In May 1996, three white teenagers were arrested and charged with burning down the church.

St. John Baptist Church was one of at least 73 African-American churches that suffered suspicious fires or acts of desecration since January 1, 1995.

While the great majority of the incidents took place in the South, other parts of the country have not been immune. For instance, in January 1994, two members of the Fourth Reich Skinheads were sentenced to prison terms for plotting an attack on the historic First African Methodist Episcopal Church in South-Central Los Angeles. The racist skinheads had hoped that the attack, which was averted by their arrest, would trigger a race war.

As the church-burnings have aroused increasing public concern, several commentators, including the editorial page of the *New York Post*, have called the issue a "hoax." While there is not definitive evidence of a national conspiracy—and civil rights advocates have not contended there is—these facts cannot be obscured:

- 73 predominantly black churches have been burned or desecrated since January, 1995.
- A *USA Today* investigation found that, although a number of white churches have burned since January 1995, the rate of black church arsons is more than double what it had been in earlier years. . . .

- The *USA Today* investigation also found "two well-defined geographic clusters or 'Arson zones' where black church arsons are up sharply over the last three years."

The zones are:

1) "a 200-mile oval in the mid-South that encompasses western Tennessee and parts of Alabama and Mississippi," and

2) another area that "stretches across the Carolinas, where the rate of black church arsons has tripled since 1993."

Of those who have been arrested or prosecuted for destroying black churches since 1990, the majority have been white males between the ages of 14 and 45. And of the 39 people who have been arrested in the arsons that occurred since January 1995, 26 have been white, 13 black. . . .

All this suggests that President Bill Clinton is correct: "We do not have evidence of a national conspiracy, but it is clear that racial hostility is the driving force behind a number of these incidents. This must stop."

As with hate crimes against other groups, acts of violence and intimidation against African-Americans are by no means confined to the destruction of houses of worship. Other examples of hate crimes against blacks include:

- On December 7, 1995, two African-American residents of Fayetteville, North Carolina, were brutally and senselessly murdered by three soldiers who apparently identified themselves as neo-Nazi skinheads. Police said the soldiers were looking for black people to harass and shot the victims as they were walking down the street. . . .

- On Friday, March 29, 1996, an African-American woman, Bridget Ward, and her two daughters, Jamila, 9, and Jasmine, 3, moved into a rented home in the virtually all-white Philadelphia neighborhood of Bridesburg. Late that night, she heard young people marching down the street, chanting, "Burn, motherf--, burn." The next morning, Ward, who works as a nurse's aide, found racial slurs smeared on her house, ketchup spilled on the front sidewalk and back porch, and an oily liquid was splattered in the rear. From Mayor Rendell to ordinary citizens, including many of Ward's neighbors, most Philadelphians were horrified by the incident. Police patrols were stepped up on the block, and the department's Crisis Prevention and Resolution Unit, which typically handles racial incidents, investigated the crime. But Ward continued to be subjected to racial harassment, including a letter threatening her and her children. Five weeks after she moved to Bridesburg, Ward announced her intention to move. The acts of racial hostility against the Ward family are typical of hate crimes intended to keep members of racial, ethnic, or religious minorities out of many neighborhoods. . . .

Attacks on Jews

Of attacks upon individuals or institutions because of their religion, the overwhelming majority—82% of such crimes reported by the FBI for 1995—were directed against Jews.

As with attacks upon African-Americans, hate crimes against Jews draw upon centuries of such assaults, from the pogroms of Eastern Europe to the Nazi Holocaust to the cross-burnings of the Ku Klux Klan in this country. Hate crimes against Jews in the United States range from physical assaults upon individuals to desecrations of synagogues and cemeteries and the painting of swastikas on private homes. . . .

Hatred against Jews is fed by slanders and stereotypes that have their origins in Europe extending back for centuries. These range far beyond the view that Jews were "Christ-killers" and include conspiracy theories involving "international bankers," the State of Israel, and groups ranging from communists to freemasons. Such views are spread by groups on the political right as well as on the left who find little basis for agreement except for their anti-Semitism. As in the past, these extremists have tried to exploit the hardships of Americans from unemployed industrial workers to hard-pressed farmers. Similarly, extremists associated with some black nationalist groups have promoted anti-Semitic conspiracy theories within the black community, exploiting the pain of poverty and discrimination and exacerbating tensions between African-Americans and Jews.

In a private survey of anti-semitic incidents [it is important to note that this survey includes hateful speech as well as hate crimes] reported to the ADL in 1995, the group found 1,843 acts against property or persons. . . . Crimes against Jews include: . . .

- On August 19, 1991, a traffic accident in Crown Heights, Brooklyn (a community with a long history of racial and religious animosity among African-Americans, Hasidic Jews, and Caribbean Nationals) resulted in the tragic death of seven-year-old African-American Gavin Cato and injury to his cousin, Angela. The driver of the car was part of Grand Rebbe Menachem M. Schneerson's motorcade. The Grand Rebbe was a religious leader of Lubavitch Hasidic Jews. A riot followed over three days during which crowds roamed the streets yelling "Get the Jews" and "Heil Hitler." Jewish-owned homes, cars, and other property were attacked. Yankel Rosenbaum, an Australian scholar, was stopped by a gang of twenty youngsters who yelled "Get the Jew." Rosenbaum was assaulted, held down, stabbed, and left bleeding on a car hood. He died. . . .
- Freddy's Fashion Mart was a Jewish-owned store in Harlem, New York, that rented space from a black church and sublet some of that space to a black-owned record store. The landlord and owner of Freddy's wanted the Fashion Mart to expand. The owner of the record store didn't want to move and a protest of Freddy's

was begun. Some people on the picket line, and their supporters, regularly engaged in anti-Semitic rhetoric. On December 8, 1995, Roland Smith, one of the protesters, entered the store with a gun and lighter fluid. He doused the store and set it on fire. Eight people—including Smith—died. Although none were Jewish, anti-semitism strife was an underlying factor.

Attacks on Hispanics

Of 814 hate crimes in 1995 that were motivated by bias based on ethnicity or national origin, 63.3%—516 in all—were directed against Hispanics.

In California and throughout the Southwest, long-existing antagonisms against Hispanics have been aggravated by the furor over immigration. . . . In November, 1994, 59% of California voters approved a statewide referendum proposal, Proposition 187, which declares undocumented immigrants ineligible for most public services, including public education and non-emergency health care.

As with attacks upon African-Americans and Jews, attacks upon Hispanics are part of a history of hatred. In California and throughout the Southwest, there have been recurring periods of "nativism," when not only newcomers but longtime U.S. citizens of Mexican descent have been blamed for social and economic problems. During the Depression of the 1930's, citizens and non-citizens of Mexican descent were the targets of mass deportations, with a half million "dumped" across the border in Mexico. In the early 1950's, a paramilitary effort, with the degrading name "Operation Wetback," deported tens of thousands of Mexicans from California and several other southwestern states. . . .

During the emotionally charged debate over Proposition 187, hate speech and violent acts against Latinos increased dramatically. And in the aftermath of the approval of 187, civil rights violations against Latinos went on the upswing, with most of the cases involving United States citizens or permanent legal residents. All in all, in the Los Angeles metropolitan area alone, the County Human Relations Commission documented an 11.9% increase in hate crimes against Latinos in 1994. . . .

- Bigotry and hate crimes against Hispanics are not confined to California and the Southwest. From the Midwest, to the Northeast, to Florida, Mexican-Americans, Puerto Ricans, Cuban-Americans, and immigrants from other countries in Central and South America have been the targets of harassment and violence.

Here are several examples of hate crimes against Hispanics over the years:

- In the summer of 1995, Allen Adams and Tad Page were sentenced to 88 and 70 months, respectively, for their roles in the ethnically motivated shooting of four Latinos in Livermore, Maine. Three of the shooting victims were migrant laborers working in an egg farm, while the fourth was visiting his ailing mother, a migrant worker. The incident began at a store, where the victims were trying to make a purchase. Adams and Page, who were also at the store, taunted the victims with ethnic epithets, telling them: "Go back to Mexico or [we'll] send you there in a bodybag." After the victims drove away from the store, Adams and Page chased them by car, firing 11 rounds from a nine-millimeter handgun at the victims' automobile. One victim was shot in the arm, while another bullet hit the driver's headrest, just a few centimeters from the driver.

• On June 11, 1995, arsonists burned down the home of a Latino family in the Antelope Valley, California, city of Palmdale. They spray-painted these messages on the walls: "White [sic] power" and "your family dies.". . .

• Hispanic rights organizations charge that Hispanic-Americans are often targets of a growing trend of abuse by private citizens and local law enforcement officials. They attribute the increasing abuse in part to the hostile political climate in which anyone who is perceived as an immigrant becomes a target for "enforcement" activities that are excessive, inappropriate, and often illegal.

Attacks on Asian Pacific Americans

Anti-immigrant sentiment also seems to be feeding attacks upon Asian-Americans. A study found that there were 461 anti-Asian incidents reported in 1995—2% more than in 1994 and 38% more than in 1993. The violence of the incidents increased dramatically, with assaults rising by almost 11%, aggravated assaults by 14%, and two murders and one firebomb attack committed. The number and severity of the incidents increased significantly in the two largest states, California and New York.

As with other minorities, violence against Asian-Americans feeds upon longstanding discrimination and contemporary tensions. Chinese, Japanese, and other Asian-Americans have been subjected to cycles of intolerance since they first arrived in the United States more than a century-and-a-half ago. . . .

In recent decades, Asian Pacific Americans have been the targets of a range of resentments. Anti-Japanese sentiments remaining from World War II have been exacerbated by the resentment of economic competition from Japan and, more recently, South Korea. Although they are likely to have supported the governments of South Vietnam, Vietnamese immigrants have been the target of Americans' shame and anger at our defeat in the war in their native land.

Since those who tend towards intolerance are often unable to distinguish one national-origin minority from another, these resentments have spilled over into hostility towards all Asian Pacific Americans. Meanwhile, for those who hate non-whites or fear immigrants and their children, Asian Pacific Americans are one more target for their free-floating rage. And these antagonisms have been aggravated by the stereotype of Asian Pacific Americans as "a model minority"—harder-working, more successful in school, and supposedly more affluent than most Americans. It is an image remarkably similar to the stereotype of Jews—a stereotype that fuels a mixture of admiration and resentment. In addition, some people do not accept Asian Pacific Americans as legitimate Americans, viewing them as perpetual foreigners.

These examples illustrate the range of hate crimes against Asian Pacific Americans:

- A 19-year-old Vietnamese-American pre-med student in Coral Springs, Fla., was beaten to death in August 1992, by a mob of white youths who called him "chink" and "Vietcong."
- On the afternoon of November 8, 1995, in the parking lot of a supermarket in Novato, California, Eddy Wu, a 23-year-old Chinese-American, was carrying groceries to his car when he was attacked by Robert Page, who stabbed him twice. Chasing Wu into the supermarket, Page stabbed him two more times. Wu suffered several serious injuries, including a punctured lung. In his confession, Page, an unemployed musician, said: "I didn't have anything to do when I woke up. No friends were around. It seemed that no one wanted to be around me. So I figured, "What the f-- I'm going to kill me a Chinaman." He also said he wanted to kill an Asian because they "got all the good jobs." Page pleaded guilty to attempted murder and a hate crime, and was sentenced to eleven years. . . .

Attacks on Arab-Americans

Especially in times of crisis in the Middle East or during incidents of domestic terrorism, the two-to-three-million Americans of Arab descent are vulnerable to hostility, harassment, and violence. But, because the federal government does not recognize Arab-Americans as a distinct ethnic group, the Justice Department does not report on how many hate crimes are committed each year against Arab-Americans.

Arab-Americans suffer from being stereotyped as everything from exotic belly-dancers to desert nomads, terrorists, religious fanatics, and oil-rich sheiks. As with Jewish-Americans and Asian-Americans, Arab-Americans are often resented by residents of communities where they run small businesses. Arab-Americans, many of whom are recent immigrants, must also deal with problems of nativism and anti-immigrant attitudes similar to that faced by Hispanics and Asian-Americans. Too often, the media blame Arabs or Muslims for incidents to which they have no connection. . . .

As with African-Americans and Jews, houses of worship are especially vulnerable. During 1995, at least seven mosques were burned down or seriously vandalized.

Illustrative of the types of hate crimes directed against Arab-Americans are:

- In Aurora, Colorado, a campus chapter of the American Arab Discrimination Committee received threatening letters and telephone calls as it sought to organize an "Arab Awareness Week." In an apparent effort to discourage the effort, the president of the chapter was assaulted on campus by two individuals.
- In Oklahoma City, following the 1995 bombing of the federal office building, an Iraqi refugee in her mid 20s miscarried her near-term baby after an April 20th attack on her home. Unknown assailants pounded on the door of her home, broke windows, and screamed anti-Islamic epithets. . . .

The Federal Response

Under the Hate Crime Statistics Act of 1990 and its extension in 1996, the Attorney General collects data on the number of crimes committed each year that are motivated by "prejudice based on race, religion, sexual orientation, or ethnicity.". . .

Meanwhile, the FBI has trained almost 3,700 staff members from almost 1,200 state, local, and federal law enforcement agencies on how to prevent, prosecute, and deal with the aftermath of hate crimes.

In these training programs, the FBI works with the Justice Department's Community Relations Service (CRS). Created by the 1964 Civil Rights Act, CRS is the only federal agency whose most important purpose is to help communities cope with disputes among different racial, religious, and ethnic groups. CRS professionals have helped with Hate Crime Statistics Act training sessions for hundreds of law enforcement officials from dozens of police agencies around the country.

In 1992, Congress approved several new programs under the Juvenile Justice and Delinquency Prevention Act to combat hate crimes and reduce racial and religious prejudice:

- Each state's juvenile delinquency plan must include a component designed to combat hate crimes.
- The Justice Department's Office of Juvenile Justice Delinquency Programs (OJJDP) is conducting a national assessment of youths who commit hate crimes, their motives, their victims, and the penalties they receive for their crimes. . . .
- OJJDP has also provided a $50,000 grant to develop a curriculum for preventing and treating hate crimes by juveniles. . . .

In the aftermath of the rash of fires at black churches, and with the strong support of the Leadership Conference on Civil Rights, Congress passed and President Clinton signed into law the Church Arsons Prevention Act of 1996. . . . It enhances federal jurisdiction over and increases the federal penalties for the destruction of houses of worship. . . .

The U.S. Commission on Civil Rights (USCCR) has undertaken a project to produce radio public service announcements on discrimination and denials of equal protection of the law. . . .

The United States has ratified two core international human rights treaties that are relevant to the problem of hate crimes. In 1992, the United States ratified the International Covenant on Civil and Political Rights, undertaking an international commitment to ensure that everyone in the U.S. enjoys the rights outlined in the treaty, including the right not to be subjected to cruel, inhuman or degrading treatment, "without distinction of any kind, such as race, color, sex, language, religion, political or other opinion, national or social origin, property, birth or other status.". . .

In 1994, the United States ratified the Convention on the Elimination of All Forms of Racial Discrimination, which places additional responsibilities on states party to the treaty to take "special and concrete measures to ensure the . . . protection of certain racial groups or individuals belonging to them, for the purpose of guaranteeing them the full and equal enjoyment of human rights and fundamental freedoms."

The State and Local Response

All of the states, with the exception of Nebraska, South Carolina, and Wyoming, and including the District of Columbia, have passed some form of hate crime statute. . . .

In addition, some states have gone further by enacting statutes that "enhance" criminal penalties for hate-motivated crimes. . . .

Another encouraging development is the founding of special bias units in a growing number of cities, including New York. (While creating the New York City unit was a positive step, there are still problems with under-reporting of hate crimes and police-community relations.) Officers in these squads are specially trained to be sensitive to victims of bias crimes. . . .

Yet another hopeful sign is the growing number of local governments that are sponsoring community education programs to reduce prejudice of all kinds and discourage hate crimes. . . .

Private Initiatives

Civil rights, religious, civic, educational, and business organizations have long played a leading role in combating bigotry and crimes motivated by bias.

For instance, since 1992, the Leadership Conference Education Fund (LCEF) has been conducting an informational campaign in partnership with the Advertising Council to promote interracial understanding and combat bigotry of all kinds. The campaign includes public service announcements in English and Spanish, with the message: "Life's too short. Stop the hate.". . .

The Anti-Defamation League has developed a number of hate

crime training resources that are available to communities and law enforcement officials. . . .

People for the American Way's STAR (Students Talk About Race) Program trains college volunteers to lead discussions in high school and middle school classrooms to provide a forum for youth to share their personal thoughts and experiences, to reflect on complex issues like prejudice and citizen responsibility, and to learn the value of tolerance in today's society.

In addition to the Southern Poverty Law Center's legal work against hate groups, its Teaching Tolerance project provides training and curriculum materials for teachers, including the *Teaching Tolerance Magazine*. . . .

In 1996, public outrage over the arsons of black churches has prompted renewed efforts to promote racial reconciliation. Private citizens, businesses, religious and civic groups have raised more than $10 million to help small congregations rebuild their church buildings. In other gestures of support, bankers have offered low-interest loans and individuals have offered to help rebuild the churches themselves. . . .

Four leading human rights groups have launched a new initiative, "Bigotry Watch," to monitor and respond to acts of intolerance of all kinds throughout the nation.

HATE CRIMES AGAINST ASIAN AMERICANS ARE INCREASING

Marie K. Shanahan

Marie K. Shanahan reports on the national increase in hate crimes that target Asian Americans—crimes motivated by prejudice and intolerance. Incidences of ethnic bias against Asian Americans have ranged from verbal threats to physical violence, Shanahan writes. She relates that the persistence of negative stereotypes of Asian Americans, combined with the rapidly growing number of Asian Americans in the United States and commonly held perceptions of their economic success, have led to increased resentment and anti-Asian feelings. Shanahan is a staff writer for the *Hartford Courant*, a Connecticut newspaper.

Even though there have been relatively few reports of hate crimes against Asian Americans in Connecticut recently, hate crimes against them are apparently on the rise nationally—from racially motivated bomb threats and physical assaults to hate-filled e-mail.

A 27-page report, released today, to U.S. Attorney General Janet Reno by the Washington-based National Asian Pacific American Legal Consortium, documents a 17 percent national increase in anti-Asian crimes in the past year.

The study is a contribution to the White House Conference on Hate Crimes, scheduled this fall as part of President Clinton's initiative on race.

Elizabeth OuYang, an attorney for the Asian American Legal Defense and Education Fund in New York City, cited a number of reasons for the growth in crimes motivated by bias and bigotry against Asian Americans.

"The climate of anti-Asian sentiment has been increasing over the years with the passing of anti-immigrant legislation," she said. "Statements made by elected politicians with respect to Asian Americans have included negative stereotypes and race-baiting related to the controversy over campaign fund contributions."

Many Asian Americans in Connecticut say negative stereotypes of them as well-mannered geniuses or perpetual foreigners contribute to the racial tensions.

Reprinted, with permission, from "Hate Crimes Against Asian Americans Are Increasing," by Marie K. Shanahan, *The Hartford Courant*, September 9, 1997.

"Just by my name a lot of people assume a lot of things," said Vikram Shenoy, 22, a senior at the University of Connecticut who is of Indian descent. "But I was born here. I grew up here, went to a small school in a small town."

Shenoy said he has encountered people who still believe in the model minority myth—"that all Asians are quiet people who excel in math and engineering."

"The stereotypes build people's rage, ignorance and jealousy," he said.

Jack Hasagawa, a Japanese American who works as an executive assistant to the state commissioner of education, agreed.

"There is a resentment against the success some Asian Americans have experienced," he said. "Couple that with high unemployment and economic downturning, and tensions worsen."

Asian Americans are the fastest growing minority group in the United States with more than 7.5 million people. In Connecticut, the population of people with Asian ancestry is expected to grow 155 percent by 2025 to about 130,000 people, according to U.S. Census figures.

"As our presence becomes more visible, it poses a threat to people," OuYang said.

Hasagawa said nothing official shows an increase in anti-Asian violence or harassment in state schools, but "there are hints it is there, boiling beneath the surface."

He said he heard recently that an Asian American student walking down the hall of a local junior high school with a white student was pushed and taunted by a group of boys saying he should "go with his own kind."

"I am aware there is tension out there, but even among multiple generation Asian Americans, there is a reluctance to come out and report bias or discrimination."

In the past three years, the state has documented seven anti-Asian hate crimes.

But OuYang warned that low numbers in places like Connecticut that don't have large concentrations of Asian Americans or community-based advocacy groups may be deceiving.

"Asian Americans may not know where to report or are afraid to. There may be a language barrier, distrust of the system," she said. "Without the support from an advocacy group to walk them through the process, they may not file a complaint."

Paul Bock, an Asian American activist who moved to Seattle after living in West Hartford for 35 years, said he believes there is an institutionalized racism against Asian Americans in the state.

He noted that Connecticut has never had an Asian American official elected to a statewide office and few Asian Americans have ever been appointed to important positions in higher education.

"We are absolutely qualified, but like a 140-pound young athlete trying out for fullback for the UConn football team, we are perceived as not having the wherewithal," said Bock, who began his activism after a 1987 incident where a group of Asian American UConn students riding a bus to an off-campus dance were taunted and spat on by white students.

"There has been a long term backlog of hatred against Asians that is taking a long time to wear off," he said.

According to the legal consortium's report, there were 534 suspected and confirmed anti-Asian incidents in the United States in 1996, reflecting a steady increase in the past four years. Among them:

- A 19-year-old former student at the University of California at Irvine allegedly sent hate mail via the Internet to nearly 60 classmates with Asian surnames.
- Six Asian American students were beaten and taunted with racial epithets by a group of white patrons at a Denny's restaurant in Syracuse, N.Y.
- A Japanese American state legislative candidate in Vancouver, Wash., received hate mail that contained a copy of his campaign letter along with epithets.

"To deal with hate crimes effectively requires an institutional response at all levels—from politicians to law enforcement to society in general," OuYang said.

SCHOOLS FACE ETHNIC CHALLENGES

Amanda Covarrubias

In the following selection, Amanda Covarrubias reports on the ethnic tension and violence challenging some Los Angeles–area schools. According to Covarrubias, as new ethnic groups move into an urban neighborhood, ethnic rivalries can develop that often are reflected in the schools, frequently resulting in controversies over such issues as staffing, curriculum, and bilingual education. Ethnic tension also can result in violence between different groups of students, she writes. Covarrubias focuses on the issue of whether or not schools should have principals and administrators of the same ethnic heritage as the majority of the students, which is a topic of heated debate in the Los Angeles school district. Covarrubias is a reporter for the *Los Angeles Daily News*.

Early in February 1999, a white principal at a mostly Hispanic elementary school was beaten up outside by two men who told him: "We don't want you here anymore, principal. Do you understand that, white principal?"

In January 1999, another Los Angeles–area school dropped its observance of both Black History Month and Cinco de Mayo after Hispanics complained they were getting only one day of attention compared with a whole month for blacks.

New Ethnic Groups, New Challenges

The two racial flare-ups illustrate the challenges faced by Los Angeles–area schools as urban neighborhoods are transformed by new ethnic groups.

"Our communities are changing quickly," said Lee Wallach, executive director of Days of Dialogue, a nonprofit conflict resolution group that led mediation talks after the attack on the principal. "L.A. is such a melting pot and so transient and these communities are changing, really monthly. When that happens and no one's talking to each other, it creates a lot of hostility."

Norman Bernstein, the 65-year-old principal at Burton Street Elementary, was beaten on Feb. 1, 1999, in an attack police are investi-

Reprinted, with permission, from "Race Tensions Flare in L.A. Schools," by Amanda Covarrubias, *Los Angeles Daily News*, February 16, 1999.

gating as a hate crime. He told police that at least one of the assailants was Hispanic. No arrests have been made.

The attack on the 40-year district veteran led to angry words among teachers, parents and administrators, who blame each other for creating a volatile atmosphere at the 750-student school, which is 90 percent Hispanic.

Burton Street Elementary is in Los Angeles' Panorama City section, in the San Fernando Valley. The neighborhood had a more even balance of whites and Hispanics back in the 1980s.

Some parents had been pushing for Bernstein's replacement by a Spanish-speaking principal. They complained he was insensitive to their concerns over Proposition 227, the state law banning bilingual education. They also accused him of trying to thwart their efforts to obtain waivers allowing their children to remain in bilingual classes.

"We just want justice for our kids," parent Lorena Aguilar said. "There are students who tell their parents they don't want to come to school. What will happen when they get to junior high or high school?"

Bernstein has not gone back to work since the attack and has not returned calls for comment.

Ability or Cultural Background?

The question of whether predominantly ethnic schools should have principals and administrators who speak the same language is at the heart of much of the tension in the 600,000-student Los Angeles district.

District leaders, as well as Mayor Richard Riordan, strongly believe administrators should be chosen on the basis of ability, not cultural background.

Some school board members disagree, siding with a growing number of ethnic parents who feel their children are best served by administrators of the same background.

Riordan has said such talk only serves to further divide the city. When School Board President Victoria Castro suggested Burton Street parents had a right to want a Spanish-speaking principal, Riordan responded angrily by saying Mrs. Castro should "wash her mouth out with soap."

A Multicultural Approach Is Needed

Just outside the city, Inglewood High School dropped both Black History Month and Cinco de Mayo for fear of the violence and student walkouts that have occurred during the past several years.

Inglewood High was once overwhelmingly black, but in a transformation that began in the late 1980s, it is now nearly 60 percent Hispanic.

In May of 1998, Inglewood High was forced to close for a day after a riot broke out and dozens of police were called in. A task force found that the fight began, in part, because Hispanic students were angry that blacks got a whole month to celebrate their heritage. Cinco de Mayo marks a May 5, 1862, victory in Mexico's battle for independence.

Principal Lowell Winston has told teachers instead to follow a "multicultural education approach" throughout the school year and "talk about all cultures and contributions all the time."

"You can't continue to do things the way they were done in the past," he said."This school has had racial problems that are unique. The old ways didn't work."

Racial Tensions Take a Toll

Back in the Los Angeles school district, three black teachers and a 13-year-old black former student at South Gate Middle School near Watts have filed a lawsuit alleging the district failed to halt discrimination against them at the school, which is more than 98 percent Hispanic vs. 63 percent back in 1978.

At Burton Street Elementary, Mia Regalado doubts her 9-year-old son Steven will learn how to read anytime soon, not with educators and parents busy trying to ease racial tensions.

Said Ms. Regalado, whose son is repeating second grade because of his inability to read: "I'm not so much concerned about race as I am about a teacher's ability to teach."

MY LIFE AS A SKINHEAD

Thomas James Leyden, as told to the Simon Wiesenthal Center

Headquartered in Los Angeles, California, the Simon Wiesenthal Center is an international center that works for the defense of human rights and to combat bigotry and anti-Semitism. Thomas James (TJ) Leyden is a former member of the neo-Nazi movement who now is working with the Wiesenthal Center's Task Force Against Hate to expose the activities of white supremacists. In the following selection, Leyden explains how he became involved with the neo-Nazi movement and became an active member of White Aryan Resistance, a white supremacist group. According to Leyden, he devoted the next few years of his life to instigating fights between whites and minorities and to recruiting young people into the movement. He describes why and how he got out of the movement and the repercussions of his decision to put his "skinhead" life behind him.

Thomas James (TJ) Leyden is a self-proclaimed former skinhead and a fifteen-year member of the neo-Nazi, White Supremacy Movement. Due to his recent and profound change of heart, Leyden abandoned the skinhead movement in an effort to redeem himself from the violence and hatred of his former lifestyle.

In an unprecedented chain of events, TJ decided to contact the Simon Wiesenthal Center with his story. . . .

TJ's biography, presented below, has been the subject of features in *Time Magazine*, *NBC Evening News*, and *The Los Angeles Times*. In addition to revealing the routine activities and beliefs of white supremacists, Leyden's story discloses the tactics neo-Nazis use to recruit new and young members. . . .

How It All Started

I grew up in a close-knit Catholic family in Fontana, California. My mother has described us as "middle America"—a working class, well-disciplined household. My brothers and I were required to be present for dinner every night and back inside by curfew. We went to church on a regular basis.

When I was 15 years old, my parents divorced. This left me angry,

Reprinted, with permission, from "The Making of a Skinhead," by Thomas James Leyden, 1999, published at the Simon Wiesenthal Center website at http://www.wiesenthal.com/tj/index.html.

lonely and most important, vulnerable. On weekends, I would escape the shouting in my home by running off to concerts where I could vent my rage by slam-dancing and fighting. I could release anger against people and they wouldn't care. Probably every show I went to, I punched someone in the face.

I now realize that I was the perfect target for neo-Nazi recruitment. Members of the white supremacy movement look for young, angry kids who need a family. I thought these were good guys, that I was being patriotic. I believed we were cleaning up America by drinking and fighting.

Soon I began wearing the trapping of the movement—Doc Marten boots, bomber jackets, a shaved head—and violent behavior. I once attacked a white youth at a party who was dating a black girl. I kicked him bloody until somebody pulled me off, grabbed a beer and joked about it. Over the years, hundreds of such fights followed and I began to earn myself the reputation as a particularly violent and militant warrior. If we saw a black or Hispanic kid on the street, we'd throw beer bottles at him or yell a racial epithet. If he yelled back at us or flipped us off, it was reason enough to stop the car, get out and beat him up.

Recruiting New Followers

When I was 21, I joined the Marines and went to the Kaneohe Bay Air Station in Hawaii. When I was off duty, I used to walk around in a tank top so people could see my tattoos. I kept my hair as short as possible and tucked my pants in my boots the way Nazis used to do. I had a Third Reich battle flag in my locker and the Confederate Stars and Bars on my wall.

While I was in Hawaii, I began associating with Tom Metzger, the founder of the White Aryan Resistance. Tom wanted more military recruits so they started sending me literature. I successfully recruited at least four other Marines by showing them videos about the White Aryan Resistance and playing them the music of bands whose lyrics preach hatred and violence. In 1990, I was discharged from the Marine Corps for "alcohol-related" behavior and questionable loyalty. I was not quiet about my involvement with the skinhead movement and its purpose.

I began corresponding with my future wife Nicole when my fellow skinheads discovered my troubles finding skinhead women in Hawaii. Nicole met me at the airport when I was discharged. We lived together two years before getting married and were heavily involved in the white supremacy movement. Nicole and I attended several Aryan Fests and even planned and organized one near Barstow, California. For several months we lived with my mother, who rejected my neo-Nazi involvement and refused to entertain our discussions concerning the Holocaust.

I dedicated most of my time to recruiting new—and young—followers for the Aryan movement. I targeted junior high schools in particular by instigating fights between white and non-white kids. Often I used the tactic of asking the white kids, "Shouldn't there be a group for you?" I passed out racial comics and Aryan Resistance leaflets to the young students and became affectionately known as "Grandpa," giving me a sense of the premature age of the children.

My Growing Discomfort

At this time, a discomfort with the movement began to grow in me. My social life was stifled by our insistence to stay at home to avoid contact with non-whites. I also realized that some of the movement's hatred could easily be directed towards my own family. My mother was left with a slight limp after suffering from polio as a child. Disabled people—even if they were white—were referred to as "surplus" when considering the future perfection of the Aryan race. My brother is a policeman. The frequent jokes about killing cops started to seem less than funny.

Nicole, however, became more deeply involved in the movement. Upon her request, we moved to the "whiter" environment of St. George, Utah, and then to Hailey, Idaho. Our marriage began to fall apart and I found myself in emotional turmoil. Our two sons kept me from hitting the edge. They also made me re-think the value of my involvement with the neo-Nazi movement. One incident specifically caused me to step back. My eldest son turned off the television when a show with African American actors aired. He told me that "we're not allowed to watch shows with niggers." I thought of the saying we often hear in the movement: "You don't want the weekend patriot—you want his kid." I realized that my sons will some day become members of the Order and murder people based on their skin color, religion or sexual preference. My kids will be sacrificed due to my example—that idea hurts. All the stuff that I had been perpetuating was coming out in my son. He's not going to be a doctor finding a cure for cancer. He's not going to be a lawyer on the Supreme Court. He's going to be a mindless bum beating people.

How I Got Out

In April 1998, I finally decided to get out of the movement. My mother convinced me to contact the Simon Wiesenthal Center after hearing about it on some television news programs. I have shared my story with the rabbis and hate group specialists at the center who have convinced me that I can help heighten awareness of the activities and recruiting tactics of hate groups. I am currently involved in a bitter custody battle for my children. I fear for my children as Nicole has stated in the past that she would kill members of her own family if they were not Aryan or part of the movement.

I realize my recent actions have put my family at risk. We frequently receive obscene phone calls, but I refuse to let these threats scare me. I was involved in this and I know things happen. I am prepared for things to come back my way. Skinheads love to hate. They feed on anger. When you're in the movement, you don't care about how much pain you inflict on anybody.

A RACIAL MURDER IN TEXAS

Howard Chua-Eoan

In the following selection, Howard Chua-Eoan describes the brutal 1998 murder of James Byrd Jr., an African American, by three young white men from Jasper, a rural East Texas town. Some local residents, writes Chua-Eoan, claim that the murder was an isolated incident in a town where, for the most part, blacks and whites live in harmony. However, he explains, others say that the area—with its legacy of the Civil War and its limited economic opportunities for young white men—is fertile ground for white supremacists. The author also notes the growing presence in the area of Christian Identity churches that preach racism and approve of ethnic violence. Whether or not the three murderers were directly involved with racist organizations, the violent murder they committed is a disturbing sign of the destructiveness of racial hatred, he concludes. Chua-Eoan is the assistant managing editor of *Time* magazine.

The Ancient Greeks told of a mania that masquerades as clarity, one that demands tearing a human being limb from limb and scattering his or her remains to the winds to quench some dire compulsion for cosmic order. That kind of bacchanalia, bloody and bestial, did not perish with the age of Sophocles. The remains of James Byrd Jr. in Jasper County, East Texas, are testament to its endurance.

Byrd's body was found on the morning of June 7, [1998] torn apart as if some wild animal had set upon it. His torso was at the side of a country road. His head and an arm were just over a mile away, ripped from his body as it hit a concrete drainage culvert. Police marked a piece of flesh here, his dentures there, his keys somewhere else—75 red circles denoting body parts and belongings along a two-mile stretch of asphalt. Fingerprints were the only key to Byrd's identity. The night before, the 49-year-old African American, on the way home from a family reunion, had apparently hitched a ride on a truck with three white men. They drove him to a wooded area, where he was beaten, chained by his ankles to the pickup and dragged down the road for at least two miles, maybe three. His body fell to pieces.

Among the remnants, someone had dropped a cigarette lighter with the Ku Klux Klan insignia.

Primal myth now intertwines with a modern one, that of the New South. In Jasper, which is 55% white and 45% black, the New South is embodied in a black mayor and a white sheriff, both of whom came swiftly forward to declare the attack an isolated, containable hate crime. "We have no Aryan Nation or K.K.K. in Jasper County," said Sheriff Billy Rowles. Mayor R.C. Horn reinforced the notion: "We don't show any animosity here. This town has been about loving each other. If it was different, I wouldn't be mayor." Residents of Jasper (pop. 7,500) loudly decried the murder; so did relatives of the suspects. Ronald King, whose son John William, 23, is in custody, wrote to a local TV station, "It hurts me deeply to know that a boy I raised . . . could find it in himself to take a life. The deed cannot be undone but I hope we can all find it in our hearts to go forward in peace and with love for all." Even the Imperial Wizard from the nearby town of Vidor sent condolences. The Klan, he wrote, had nothing to gain from the "senseless tragedy."

But some citizens were not persuaded by the protestations of harmony. "How deep does this river run?" asked Herman Wright, an African American and the manager of a local sawmill. The remarks by Sheriff Rowles were greeted with hoots. In Jasper, people still wonder about the suicide a few years back of a popular black high school football player who dated a white girl. People ask, though without evidence, Did he really hang himself, or was he lynched? And just two weeks ago, a white youth was beaten up by black teens.

Everyone knows everyone else in Jasper. Byrd may have been invited to hitch a ride by one suspect, the truck's owner, Shawn Allen Berry, 23, with whom he shared a parole officer. (Byrd had served time for theft and forgery, Berry for burglary.) The Byrd and King families have been in Jasper for generations. A member of Byrd's extended family had worked as a babysitter for a relative of King's. And yet, if what Berry told police is accurate, his friend King was openly hostile to Byrd and, while beating him, allegedly said he was "starting *The Turner Diaries* early," a reference to the antigovernment-conspiracy novel that is a must-read for white supremacists.

"Don't go reading far more into this than these guys deserve," says Rife Kimler, a local attorney. "These are three guys who got mean, got drunk and saw an easy target." But a target for what kind of anger? History lies in wait in the woods that stretch 100 miles through East Texas to Louisiana, biding its time to strike. Towns like Jasper were the refuge for Confederate deserters who fled to the forests after the Civil War. The area became fertile ground for the Klan. "There is a predisposition, a culture over here in East Texas," says John Craig, co-author of *Soldiers of God*, a new book about America's white supremacists. "It does not express itself all the time, but it is rampant over here." An all-white militia group, he says, operates a 200-acre training facility in the county. Even Kimler acknowledges that "there is a lot of quiet support for the Klan."

More worrisome is the fact that Christian Identity churches have begun springing up around Jasper, including one in nearby Burkeville. The ideology, which preaches that white people are the true Israelites, has moved in subtly. "They look for small autonomous country churches with no debt and a bank account," says Craig. "They fire the pastor, they get tax status and what looks like the Shady Grove Baptist Church; well, they are singing Amazing Grace and then saying Sieg Heil." Killing in the name of religious and racial purity is within the moral contract of Christian Identity, say experts. Authorities last week were checking if any of the three suspects had associated with the area Christian Identity churches.

The pedigree of prejudice often leads through prison. Berry and King served time on the same burglary charge. It was in prison that they met the third suspect, Lawrence Russell Brewer, 31. Says Bill Hale of the Texas Human Rights Commission: "If someone has a predisposition to racism, it will be reinforced in prison." King was involved in a racial disturbance between Anglo and Hispanic prisoners in 1995. The *Houston Chronicle* reported last week that he sent letters from prison proclaiming race hatred and allegiance to the Aryan Brotherhood, a white-supremacist gang founded in California's San Quentin State Prison in the 1960s. Texas prison officials declared that the tattoo found on Berry indicates membership in a white-supremacist organization. An ex-general of the Aryan Brotherhood sniffed that his group would never have recruited petty thieves like King, Berry and Brewer: "We recruit criminals."

But hatred does not need organization to destroy. "Ninety to 95% of hate crimes are not committed by hate groups," says Brian Levin, director of the Center on Hate and Extremism in Pomona, N.J. The local economy around Jasper is not good, and young white men there see minorities compete against them for jobs with what they perceive as unfair advantages, including affirmative action and other government programs. Many lumber mills and poultry-processing plants have recently turned to Hispanic workers, adding a new ingredient to the racial pot.

All that helps feed into what some authorities see as a decentralized, amorphous white-supremacy movement, drawing on what Levin calls the "elastic pool of disenfranchised white males who are susceptible to the message of the hate movement." He explains, "It's a do-your-own-thing franchise" that no longer needs the old Klan structure.

And what did all this mean on a night in June? "This was an opportunity crime," says Craig, as simple as finding a black man alone on a country road, as simple as having a chain in a truck to drag that man down that country road, as simple as cowardice buoyed by beer, as simple as a majority, a band of three against one. As simple as all that and yet as complex as horror.

When Byrd's sisters heard he had been killed, they thought he had been shot. Like ritualistic Fates, they went to his apartment to find his best clothes, to lay him out as splendidly as could be for one final viewing. Then the family learned what had happened. There was nothing of their brother left to see.

CHAPTER 4

ETHNIC VIOLENCE IN EUROPE

Contemporary Issues
Companion

Bosnia: An Ethnic Battleground

Chuck Sudetic

Chuck Sudetic is a political analyst for the International Crisis Group. Between 1990 and 1995, he was a journalist for the *New York Times*, covering the collapse of Yugoslavia and the war in Bosnia. In the following selection from his book *Blood and Vengeance: One Family's Story of the War in Bosnia*, Sudetic paints a vivid picture of physical and psychological damage resulting from ethnic war. He describes the search he undertook at the request of his wife, a Yugoslav Serb, to find a Muslim laborer whose son was married to her sister. Through the story of his search, Sudetic illustrates the horrors, abuses, and depravations inflicted by the war. He also relates that as a result of his contacts with his sister-in-law's husband and family, he became unable to remain emotionally detached to the human suffering in the region. He writes that he slowly began to acknowledge and respond to the personal dimension, to the hardships experienced by the victims of the war between the Bosnian Serbs and Muslims.

The opening months of the second year of the war in Bosnia, May and June of 1993, seemed to be a season for promises, big and small. I was in Sarajevo one evening late in that season when I remembered I had an appointment at a government building in the city's center and had to get there to keep a promise I had given my wife weeks earlier. The appointment had nearly slipped my mind, and I was irritated that it hadn't. I was tired. A drizzle hung in the air. And now I had to drag myself out of my room and try to make contact by ham radio with someone I knew but felt little connection with. The radio operators had postponed the appointment twice already. Drumming up some excuse to postpone it again would have been easy, and I've forgotten why I didn't.

I was making, and keeping, few personal promises back then. From a Cleveland suburb bursting with kids and housewives and working fathers, I had found my way into a mercenary, monomaniacal existence and had shoved family obligations to the bottom of my list of priorities. It was my fifth year in Yugoslavia, and I was making my living by reporting about the war for the *New York Times*. There were many incentives for staying on the road, for staying in Bosnia to work. I earned real money only if I found stories that got into print, and in all the world Bosnia was the place to find compelling stories. But it was not only the money that kept me going back. Even in peacetime, back before the war when I was a student in Yugoslavia, traveling through Bosnia's mountains had been an adventure for me, a journey back in time through the legacies of three extinct empires, one Islamic, one Eastern Orthodox, one Roman Catholic; a journey into a world run by a bankrupt Communist mafia and its secret police; a journey through wild natural beauty into a moribund world of semiliterate, hard-drinking peasant men, a world of superstitions, tattooed women, and a cult of the dead, a world where living memories and bedtime stories merged history into the landscape itself. Once the war began, there was an addictive, groin-tingling excitement to working in Bosnia. I relished the hunt for stories and words that would show the horror and the scandalous injustice of the destruction of Bosnia and the war's primary victims, the Muslims. This was easy enough. But I always felt that my stories and words failed to plumb the deep structure of Bosnia itself, especially peasant Bosnia, lumpen Bosnia, the Bosnia the war had ravaged most.

Staying Detached from the Reality of War

There is a method to presenting the reality of war in *Times* style, a restrictive method but a perfectly valid one just the same. It focuses mainly on institutions and political leaders and their duties and decisions, while leaving the common folk to exemplify trends, to serve as types: a fallen soldier, a screaming mother, a dead baby—literal symbols. . . . This method is described by various terms: detachment, disinterestedness, dispassion, distancing, and others with negative prefixes engineered to obliterate any relationship between observer and observed. When I went to Bosnia to work, I used to imagine I had entered a great grassland teeming with life. "I build a tower hundreds of feet high," I told one of my friends. "I climb it every morning and observe the wildlife devouring one another and struggling to survive down below. And from that distance, I write about what I see, send my story, have something to eat, and go to sleep." I once walked through a town littered with the purple-and-yellow bodies of men and women and a few children, some shot to death, some with their heads torn off, and I felt nothing; I strolled around with a photographer, scratched notes, and lifted sheets covering the bodies of dead men to see if they had been castrated; I picked up a white flag from the ground near the twisted bodies of half a dozen men in civilian clothes who had been shot next to a wall, and then I carried the flag home and hung it above my desk. I once saw soldiers unload babies crushed to death in the back of a truck and immediately ran off to interview their mothers. I accidentally killed an eighteen-year-old man who raced in front of my car on a bike; his head was smashed; I held the door when they loaded him into the backseat of the automobile that carried him to the emergency room of Sarajevo's main hospital. I expressed my condolences to his father; then I got a tow back to my hotel, went to my room, and sent that day's story to New York.

My observation tower had begun to wobble by then, but I managed to maintain a distance for another eighteen months, and no one could have kept me from going back to the war. It was exhilarating. It was my addiction, my mania. It even simplified life and gave it meaning. Only when I traveled home to my wife and daughters in Belgrade did the pent-up stress and anger and guilt erupt. I would slam doors, smash dishes, and swear for a few days, lobotomize myself with rented videos for a week or so, and head back to Bosnia to detach myself from my family and emotions and take up the hunt for stories and words for another month or two.

The Hunt for Huso Čelik

I had already filed my story on that drizzly Sarajevo evening in June 1993 when I remembered my appointment and my promise to my wife, Ljiljana. I had told her before I left Belgrade that I would do my best during that trip to Bosnia to track down a man named Huso Čelik, a Muslim man with crossed eyes, a laborer in the brickyard of a construction company whom I had met twice in Sarajevo before the war. There was a family connection. Ljiljana is a native Yugoslav, a Serb born and raised in Belgrade; her only sister, Gordana, had married Huso Čelik's eldest son, Hamed. No one had heard from Huso or the rest of his family since they disappeared in the Bosnian mountains during the opening months of the war. Anger, uncertainty, and a thirst for vengeance were poisoning Hamed's mind. A few months after the war began, he was fired from his job in Belgrade; a couple of days later, one of his Serb neighbors threatened to shoot him because he was a Muslim; then he left Gordana and their children and went to Austria to live with his uncle and await an immigration visa to Canada. Muslim refugees passing through Austria brought Hamed tales of the war and rumors about his family. They said a Serb gang led by a man named Milan Lukić, a school chum of Hamed's younger brother, had driven out all the Muslims from his family's hamlet. They said Hamed's father had died of a heart attack, his youngest brother had been killed, and his sister wounded. Soon Hamed's relatives and their Muslim neighbors in Austria were cackling about Hamed's Serb wife. In Belgrade, the Serbs started asking why Hamed had left his wife alone to wrestle with three kids in one room of her mother's two-room apartment.

I knew hundreds of similar stories, and after the first dozen or so they were hardly news. In that first year of the war, nationalist Serb gunmen bent on dismembering Bosnia had uprooted hundreds of thousands of Muslims and killed tens of thousands more, the vast majority of them civilians and prisoners. The survivors were scattered all over Yugoslavia and the rest of Europe. I had made an effort to ask around for Huso in refugee shelters. I inquired with government officials and occasionally scanned lists of the displaced and the dead. Some nights, I tuned in to local radio talk shows dedicated solely to greetings and messages from callers searching for their lost relatives; but this was like listening to someone read a telephone book. Finally, a friend in the government set up a time slot for me to speak by ham radio with a man named Huso Čelik who had turned up in a place called Srebrenica, a town just inside Bosnia's border with Serbia.

When I walked out of the drizzle and into the government building, a security guard pointed me toward the radio room. I figured the radio operators were not going to give me much time, so I rehearsed my questions as I climbed a staircase and set off down an empty corridor. The Serb army besieging Sarajevo had cut off the city's running water, and the air in the corridor was sticky with the odor of the shit that had piled up in the toilets all day. I found my way through the stench to an alcove where an antenna cable emerged from under a closed door, ran across the corridor, and climbed out through an open window. The radio operators asked me to wait outside for a few minutes, and I leaned out the window to breathe. "First," I thought, "I have to make sure it's the right Huso Čelik."

Trapped in Srebrenica

The operators already had Srebrenica on the air when they called me into the room. The tuner had a piece of paper covering it to hide the frequency. A garbled voice I would never have recognized emerged from the ether.

"Hallo," I said. ". . . over."

More garble I could not understand came through the crackling speaker.

"Hallo. Hallo. Where are you from? Over."

". . . up . . . sovići."

It sounded right.

"Where do you work? Over."

"Vr . . . nica. Vra . . . ca."

It was Hamed's father, all right. Vranica was the name of the construction company where Hamed had taken me to meet his father a few weeks before the war. When the signal cleared up, Huso wasted no time rattling off each family member's name. Hamed's mother, Hiba, was well. His sister had never been wounded. His brother was alive. I passed along regards from everyone in the outside world.

"Tell them we're alive and well," Huso said. "If you can, come and see us."

"I'll try," I answered, though I knew even then I would never make it.

"And bring cigarettes," Huso said, "only cigarettes."

"I understand."

"And please, try and get us out of here."

The radio operators motioned that my time was up, and we signed off. Sarajevo had no telephone links with the outside world then, so I sent a sparse message over a satellite to the *Times*'s foreign desk in New York before getting something to eat and going to sleep. My friends in New York forwarded it to Ljiljana in Belgrade so that she could call Hamed with the good news that the Čeliks were alive and the bad news that they were trapped in a town that had become something worse than a concentration camp.

I had spent much of that spring writing about how the army of the Bosnian Serbs had goaded tens of thousands of displaced Muslims into Srebrenica, battered them with artillery, demanded their surrender, and threatened to massacre the town's menfolk once the place fell. The ambassadors of the countries sitting on the United Nations Security Council had saved Srebrenica from a bloodbath by hastily declaring it to be a "safe area" and by pledging to protect it with NATO jets if the Serbs attacked again. This was the biggest promise of that season.

Srebrenica Falls

Two years later, in June of 1995, one of many seasons for broken promises arrived in Bosnia. Huso and the other Čeliks were still trapped in Srebrenica, living off humanitarian aid, smoking home-grown tobacco and pumpkin leaves, waiting out the war. Hamed had made it to Canada with Gordana and their three children; he had tried to slip cash inside Polaroid snapshots enclosed in Red Cross letters he sent to Huso from Toronto, but all of the money was stolen. Ljiljana and I had been back in New York with our two daughters for five months by then; I had exhausted myself in Bosnia, took a staff job with the *Times* that promised a secure future, and made the mistake of assuring my wife I could set the unresolved question of the war on a shelf beside my white flag and live happily in an ocean-front apartment, with weekends free for romping on the beach and trying to catch the Browns and the Indians on television.

Word of the Serb army's attack on Srebrenica came to us on the television news. Hamed glued himself to CNN around the clock and called me a few times during the five days of the offensive to see if I knew anything more than the television was reporting. The UN was releasing precious little of what it knew about the attack. I remember hearing and reading speculation by UN officials that the Serb army was only trying "to squeeze" the Srebrenica "safe area." I recognized the scent of the cheap red herring that had been dragged around Bosnia for years already by UN diplomats and military officers to cover up the sticky odor of the powerful nations of the Security Council breaking their word. Hamed and I swore together in rage. We predicted what would happen; anyone who knew page one about Bosnia could have predicted what would happen. We waited to see who would make it out alive.

A few hours after Srebrenica's fall, Serb soldiers had thousands of the town's Muslim women, children, and old people surrounded on the grounds of a decrepit battery factory next to a UN military base. The soldiers had arrived at the factory amiably enough. They gave Muslim children cookies, pieces of candy, and chunks of bread. One Serb even kissed his former neighbor on the cheeks before he escorted him away. Gunshots rang out. Women wailed. Soon the place was reeking of shit and urine. Soldiers on horseback began herding the crowd into a tighter circle. Women who went to fetch water spotted the bodies of dead boys in a creek. German shepherd dogs chased down men who had bolted into the nearby woods. One woman hung herself inside a factory building.

Huso and Hiba knew the Serb gunmen who led away a dozen of their neighbors from back home. Two of the Serbs had grown up in villages just down a dirt road from the Čelik place. Their leader, a lean, good-looking young man who was wearing a tight black shirt and baggy fatigues with a long knife in a scabbard hanging from his belt, had been the schoolmate of Hamed's younger brother. It was Milan Lukić. He assured Huso and the other Muslim men that every-thing would be fine. He said he had chartered a special bus for the Muslims from his district and picked out a dozen of them to come and get the tickets for everyone else. Huso believed Lukić. Huso even volunteered to go along with the rest of the Muslim men when Lukić and the other Serbs led them away. "I'm ready to go right now," Huso said. But the Serbs told Huso to sit down.

He shuffled back into the crowd and bundled himself up inside a worn-out army jacket as if he were freezing in the summer heat. He lit a cigarette, then griped about pains in his chest and swelling in his legs. Hiba was irritated with him. She was afraid the women nearby in the crowd would see him paralyzed with fear and hear him whining like a child. She assured him that everything would be fine. She told him they were not alone.

Reunion with the Čeliks

In September of 1995, at the beginning of a new season for promises in Bosnia, I took a month's leave from my job in New York and trav-eled back to Bosnia to meet the Čeliks who survived the slaughter at Srebrenica, the largest mass killing in Europe since the Communists took over Yugoslavia after World War II. I brought them a wad of cash, cartons of Marlboro, a stack of Canadian immigration forms, and suitcases stuffed with clothes, shoes, and toys. I also came to collect the Čeliks' memories for a story for *Rolling Stone* magazine about how the UN and the powerful countries of the world had ignored their promises and abandoned the Muslims of Srebrenica to the Serbs' tender mercies.

We talked for days in the kitchen of a gritty farmhouse, swatting mosquitoes and sipping coffees and colas and an occasional plum brandy. The Čeliks spoke with hardly a pause, and I found it strange that it was taking so long to tell the stories. Slowly I realized this was because their stories carried me far beyond a chronology of a massacre and an international scandal. The stories flashed me back to a time before the Čeliks groped their way through the mountains to Srebrenica. The stories told of a life along a troubled border long before the Bosnian war. They described a hamlet with a funny name and wives with no husbands and sons with no fathers. They spoke of a weather-beaten schoolhouse, a man with a hidden cannon, beehives that flew through kitchen windows, and a woman who galloped around on a tree branch to remove a hex from a mad cow. They turned back time to another war, and another; to invasions and rebellions; to heretics, dervishes, pashas, and sultans; to slaves and sharecroppers and a swindler with three wives. When I started talking with Serbs from around Srebrenica and the villages near the Čeliks' old home, I realized their stories dovetailed with the Muslims' and also began with memories of a time long before the war, memories of fistfights, funerals, and feasts, of great-great-grandfathers who struggled to be free of feudalism, of great-grandfathers who helped ignite a world war, and of grandfathers who fought to survive Fascist butchery, who exacted blood vengeance to appease their dead, and who suffered defeat and buried their guns for another day.

Here was the deep structure. Here, with a myriad of characters and contradictions, were images of the peasant Bosnia destroyed by the war; images that were not symbols . . . but portraits of people, of individuals, going about their lives in quiet desperation; . . . images that gave a glimpse of how peasant Bosnia had come to be, how it survived the seasons and the centuries and the wars, how it struggled to lift itself from poverty and ignorance, how its bitter, living memories were stirred as the Communist world collapsed, and how a small group of men bent on taking and keeping personal power ignited its passions and blew a country apart.

The old addiction, my mania, seized me once again, and I broke the promise I had made my wife. Within a few months I had quit my job and we had packed our apartment into a storage warehouse in Cleveland and moved back to our old neighborhood in Belgrade. I took off alone for one last stint in Bosnia for the sake of a few stories and words that might lay some living memories of the dead and of a dying world silently to rest.

CROATIA: DOES THE THREAT OF "ETHNIC CLEANSING" REMAIN?

Marc Champion

In 1991, as the country of Yugoslavia dissolved into warfare, ethnic Croatians were driven out of the region of Eastern Slavonia by local Serbs and the Yugoslav army. The region was then proclaimed to be "cleansed" of all ethnic Croats. However, by January 1998, United Nations peacekeepers were preparing to hand control of the region back to the Croatian government. Writing shortly before the transfer of power was to take place, Marc Champion warns that the threat of additional ethnic cleansing remains. According to Champion, the international community hopes to prove that the Croats can be successfully reintegrated into Eastern Slavonia, but much tension remains between the Croats and the Serbs. At issue, he states, is how many Serbs will stay in the area when thousands of displaced Croatians return and whether these Croatians take revenge on the Serbs who do stay. Champion, a freelance writer based in Moscow, Russia, covered the war in Bosnia in 1991 for the *Independent.*

The new history textbook issued to schoolchildren in Croatia this semester poses the following questions to twelve-year-old students: Who conducted the war against Croatia? What did the Greater Serbian aggressors do during the war? And what crimes did the Greater Serbian aggressors commit? For the Serb children in this bucolic Danube region where the Yugoslav wars began, the answers to these questions would be rather awkward, something like: "My father conducted the aggression." Not surprisingly, when the Serb kids brought the new books home, their parents became apoplectic. They refused to send their sons and daughters back to school until the books were withdrawn. Four hand grenades were even tossed at primary school buildings. (No one was hurt.)

In the former Yugoslavia nothing, it turns out, is easy or exactly promising. Six years after the war in eastern Croatia, history books are designed not to teach ethnic tolerance or what actually happened.

They are designed to teach who is boss. And the boss in eastern Croatia is about to change—hence the new books.

On January 15, 1998, the last blue-helmeted United Nations peacekeepers are to be pulled out. On that day, the Croatian government will regain full control of eastern Croatia for the first time since local Serbs and the Yugoslav Army brutally drove out the Croatian population in 1991. January 15 will therefore be a day of triumph for Croatian President Franjo Tudjman, who will have successfully reversed his country's last territorial loss from the war. But the departure of the United Nations Transitional Administration for Eastern Slavonia (UNTAES) will also begin a difficult test for Croatia.

"Ethnic Cleansing": Croats vs. Serbs

In 1995, Croatia—with a silent nod of approval from the United States and its allies—retook the lost enclaves of Krajina and Western Slavonia in massive military offensives, driving out the entire Serb population. Ironically, this has made the Croats, and not the Serbs, the only sure winners to date in the barbarous game called "ethnic cleansing." Two years later, Croatia is still blocking efforts to return Serb refugees to their homes. Could Eastern Slavonia be next on the list for "cleansing"?

Western officials say they're confident the answer is no. Just days before the primary school bombings, officials were celebrating the second anniversary of the U.N.-brokered agreement—an agreement that set up the UNTAES mandate in 1995 and saved Serbs here from the fates of their ethnic brothers in Krajina and Western Slavonia. "Not any place else has the peace process significantly reversed ethnic cleansing, but it's happening here," the outgoing United States ambassador to Croatia, Peter Galbraith, told me at the celebration. Indeed, with a multiethnic state in Bosnia still an illusion, Eastern Slavonia offers the international community its best chance to reintegrate a "cleansed" population in former Yugoslavia.

The great advantage here is that the dominant (Croatian) authorities will be trying to relocate their own (ethnically Croatian) people into the region. In Bosnia and elsewhere in Croatia, it is the United Nations or NATO that has to try to persuade the authorities to allow expelled minorities back in. A much tougher proposition.

Return of the Croats

There are between 120,000 and 140,000 people in the UNTAES region now, and almost all of them are Serbs. With the police under Croatian control, Zagreb should have relatively little trouble returning the 74,000 Croats it says were displaced by the war. The real question is, how many Serbs will stay? Success is vital to the international community, whose record in ex-Yugoslavia will be judged largely on whether it proves that "ethnic cleansing" doesn't work.

And despite the U.N. and U.S. declarations of victory, they may be going home too soon. Three days after their celebration, leaflets appeared in the streets of Vukovar, the quaint riverside town that the Yugoslav Army reduced to rubble during an 80-day siege in 1991. "Serbs," the leaflets read, "it is exactly 11:55. There are only two months until January 15. From December 1 we are putting you into a reservation. We like to hunt wild animals. . . . We are going to kill slowly and quietly, but not tenderly . . . a debt is a debt." The date was well chosen. On December 1, the UNTAES-trained Temporary Police Force changed into Croatian uniforms.

Some Croats will return to Dalj, a village on the Danube just a few miles upstream from Vukovar, which was traditionally mixed but has been pure Serb since the ethnic cleansing of 1991. I joined a table at a popular bar called Medison, thinking that here, if anywhere, I would find people too young to have been poisoned for the future. But no sooner had I sat down than Raiko, 23, and Iovica, 28, began pulling up their pant legs and shirts to show off their war wounds. Between 1991 and 1995, Iovica was shot three times and Raiko five. In a few months, could Raiko and Iovica be sitting here comparing wounds with young Croats? There are some causes for optimism. Zagreb has made all the right promises about nondiscrimination, amnesty, human rights, and the restoration of property. Branimir Glavas, the Croatian tough who ran the regional capital of Osijek while at least nine prominent Serbs were assassinated and 18 villagers were massacred, was at last forced to resign in October 1997.

The Animosity Still Exists

In Dalj, most Serbs said they would stay for now. But then Dalj is a fairly secure village with its own local authority. Other villages, closer to large Croatian population centers, are already emptying. Iovica, who comes from Tenja, just outside Osijek, was unconvinced. "We'll leave when the U.N. troops leave," he said as he fingered a huge ruffled scar across his abdomen. His family has already bought a house in Serbia. By the time the Croats take control of Tenja, he said, it will be virtually empty.

There are plenty of reasons for Serbs to be nervous about Zagreb's intentions, even without the anonymous leaflet campaign. Glavas, though deposed from the top job in Osijek, remains in the city as—of all things—the head of relations between the Croatian Army and civilians. And loopholes in the amnesty law have left all Serbs "wondering if we're not on some [war crimes] list," said Stevan Babich, the mayor of Dalj.

And then there are those school textbooks. Under pressure, the Croatian authorities have agreed to withdraw them, defusing the crisis temporarily. But ethnically Croatian children in the region will still be reading a poem from their Croatian language textbook that begins "I'm a little Croat" and goes on to describe the fathers of their Serbian schoolmates in Dalj as child-murderers. All of which suggest that the international community will have to keep a close watch on eastern Croatia after January 1998 if another round of "ethnic cleansing" is not to become the next chapter in Croatia's history.

THE BITTER STRUGGLE BETWEEN SERBS AND ALBANIANS

Michael T. Kaufman

In the following selection, journalist Michael T. Kaufman describes the historical roots of the struggle between Serbs and Albanians in the Balkan region of Europe. The two groups, he maintains, have strong opposing viewpoints regarding the province of Kosovo, the center of their most current violent conflict. Kaufman explains that the Serbs consider Kosovo their holy land, especially because it contains the battleground that was the site of both their worst defeat and greatest victory in their 500-year struggle against the Ottoman Turks. However, he says, the Albanians believe they have a right to Kosovo because their ancestors settled there centuries before the Serbs and because far more Albanians than Serbs actually live in Kosovo. According to Kaufman, the ethnic differences between the Serbs and the Albanians—who speak different languages, follow different religions, and dress in different types of clothing—also add to their enmity.

The conflict between Serbs and Albanians, currently embodied by the sight of Albanian families desperately fleeing Serbian pursuers in Kosovo, has a very long history that is deeply felt, if selectively recalled, by those condemned to live it. At the same time it has never been much understood or appreciated beyond the southern Balkans.

In 1780 while Edward Gibbon, the British historian, was sailing down the Adriatic and regarding the high peaks of the southeastern shore, he wrote that here was an area lying "within sight of Italy, which is less known than the interior of America." Yet, as the contemporary British historian Norman Davis has observed, no lands have "suffered more from the whims of international politics."

In the twentieth century alone, the Serbs and Albanians have had to contend with Turkish, Nazi and Italian forces of occupation, while also contending with and confronting each other. Since 1987, when Slobodan Milosevic, now the Yugoslav President, first began exploit-

Reprinted, with permission, from "Two Distinct Peoples with Two Divergent Memories Battle over One Land," by Michael T. Kaufman, *The New York Times*, April 4, 1999. Copyright ©1999 by The New York Times.

ing and inflaming the historical rivalries of Albanians and Serbs, many observers predicted that Kosovo could well become the site of the deadliest violence seen in Europe since World War II.

In 1999, as NATO's bombs fall and long lines of refugees straggle over mountain passes, the issues pitting Serbs against Albanians, which preoccupied and bedeviled the European powers for the latter part of the 19th century, have once again grown beyond the crenelated landscape of mountains and valleys.

Stimulated by Milosevic's policies, Serbs and Albanians have retreated to their own distinct politics, sharpening the differences in their already diverging historical accounts of Kosovo and the region.

Until the recently provoked flight of Albanian families, there were 1.8 million Albanians in Kosovo, the province of Serbia where ethnic Albanians accounted for 90 percent of the population.

Opposing Views of History

In general, the Serbian view of Kosovo could be summarized as follows: It is the nation's holy land, first settled by their ancestors in the seventh century. Medieval Serbian kings were crowned there. Important shrines of the Serbian Orthodox church still dot the landscape.

Most important, it was the site of the battle of Kosovo Polje, where in 1389 the Turks defeated the Serbs and set the nation on its course of 500 years of resistance to Ottoman rule. This event is at the heart of the Serbian national myth, and as the writer Noel Malcolm observed in his book, *Kosovo, a Short History,* Serbian writers have often compared the loss at Kosovo to the crucifixion of Christ, and its reconquest in 1912 to resurrection.

To the extent that a Serbian view takes account of Albanians at all, the Albanians are portrayed as having sided with or served the Ottoman Turks, and they are said to have taken over properties left behind when Serbs fled northward, particularly in the 17th and 18th centuries. The Serbs claim that in the years of Ottoman rule, the Turks favored the Albanians, most of whom are fellow Muslims, installing them as landlords and allowing them to exploit and humiliate Serbs.

Albanians see things differently. They claim that their ancestors, the ancient Illyrian tribes, who provided fighting legions for the Greek and Roman empires, were in Kosovo for centuries when the Serbs first arrived from what is now southern Poland. Moreover, they claim that Albanians had a long record of fighting the Turks, and that in fact Albanians had fought as allies of the Serbs at Kosovo Polje. They point out that their national hero, Scanderbeg, spent 20 years in the 15th century warring against the Ottoman Sultan.

The Albanians, who did not have their own state until 1913, stress that they are an overwhelming majority in the area and that they have attained such numerical supremacy despite longstanding efforts of governments in Belgrade to displace them, among these an attempt in 1926 to sponsor Serb settlements. The Albanians recall how in the period between the two world wars mosques were seized, land was confiscated, old deeds invalidated and some Albanians were forcibly put on trains and deported to Turkey.

At the moment, by their conduct in the skies over Serbia, it seems clear that the great Western powers have found the Albanians' case persuasive. But in Kosovo itself it is the Serbian view of history that is gaining ground.

Two Very Different Peoples

Despite living in close proximity over the ages, Albanians and Serbs are quite different from each other. In the case of the recent fighting in Bosnia, Eastern Orthodox Serbs, Bosnian Muslims and Catholic Croats had different religions but spoke the same language. The Serbs and Albanians are linguistically alien. Albanian is not a Slavic tongue nor does it have recognizable links to any other European language. Seventy-five percent of Albanians are Muslim, with the remainder divided between Orthodox and Catholic.

Though the young Albanians of Pristina, the Kosovo capital, would be indistinguishable in dress from their Serbian counterparts in Belgrade, their elders often still maintain distinctive garb, with men prizing flowing mustaches or wearing white felt conical caps. In Albania, particularly in the north, clans remain extremely important in determining who can and cannot be married and blood feuds are still carried out under an ancient code called the law of Lek. Currently, there are eight million to nine million Serbs, most living in Yugoslavia's two republics, Serbia and Montenegro. There are also a few Serbs in Croatia and Macedonia. There are virtually none in Albania.

As for the Albanians, some six million live where they have for generations, in what are now three contiguous countries. There are close to four million in Albania, a very poor country that in Albanian is called "Shqiperia," which means "land of the sons of the eagle." In Macedonia, the number of Albanians is officially given as half a million, or 23 percent of the population.

Such figures make these two peoples rather sizable in terms of Balkan demographics. Both Albanians and Serbs are outnumbered by Greeks, but they are more numerous than the Croats, Slovenes, Macedonians, Montenegrins and Bosnians.

The Albanian birth rate has been high everywhere, and in Kosovo it is the highest in Europe. There, 70 percent of the Albanians were under 30 years of age. Very high birth rates have also been recorded in Albania proper and among the Albanians of Macedonia. Meanwhile in Yugoslavia, the non-Albanian population has been steadily falling.

The Milosevic government has cited the statistics to arouse the Serbian population. In July 1998, for example, Serbia's Minister for Family Affairs, Rada Trajkovic, a former doctor in Pristina, called Albanian women "child-bearing machines" who she claimed did not always know the names of all their children.

A National Rebirth

Such reports have reinforced Serbian fears that while their nation has been thwarted in its dreams of securing a Greater Serbia, it may yet find itself confronted by a populous Greater Albania consisting of all the territory where Albanians form majorities. . . .

Many historians consider the Albanians, regardless of where they live, to be the last of the European peoples to be undergoing the sort of national resurgence through which much of Europe passed in the wake of the Napoleonic era.

What is called the "Albanian national awakening" began in 1878. As the Congress of Berlin was about to convene to discuss a remapping of the Balkans as Ottoman power was receding, a group of Albanians based in Prizren, in Kosovo, wrote to Benjamin Disraeli, the British Prime Minister at the time, to urge that Albanian interests be considered.

The effort was crushed when the German Chancellor, Otto von Bismarck, flatly declared that there was "no such thing as an Albanian nationality." But the Albanian Question, meaning what should be done with this distinct group of people then aspiring to have its own nation state, had been placed on the table.

The Albanian Question

Over the next three decades, as Albanians struggled against Ottoman rule, the debate raged. In 1908 they met and chose the Latin script over either cyrillic or Arabic letters, and demanded that schools teach in Albanian rather than Turkish. There were several armed uprisings to challenge the Ottomans, and by 1911 the Albanians were in full-scale rebellion. The following year, the combined armies of Serbia, Bulgaria and Greece drove Turkish forces back to the walls of Constantinople in what became known as the First Balkan War.

In the ensuing peace talks in London in 1913, the great powers agreed on the creation of an Albanian state as an independent sovereign hereditary principality with a prince to be chosen later. They also did not get around to setting the country's northern border with Serbian Kosovo, something that was not done until 1926.

Meanwhile, the anti-Ottoman alliance collapsed over territorial claims and Bulgaria attacked both Serbia and Greece in the Second Balkan War. In the fighting, Serbia, which long craved an Adriatic port, sent forces into Albania. The Austro-Hungarians who were in control of Croatia and feared such encroachment sent an ultimatum to Serbia, and when—in a prelude to World War I—the Austrians were backed up by the German Kaiser, the Serbs reluctantly withdrew.

Finally, the European powers selected Wilhelm du Zeid, a 35-year-old army captain, to be Albania's ruling Prince. He arrived in March 1914, and left six months later without establishing control over much of the turbulent country, which for years continued to be wracked by anarchy.

For much of the next seven decades, for Albania proper, it was not Serbs who would pose their greatest problems. After a period of internal skirmishing came the rule of Ahmet Zogu, who proclaimed himself King Zog. Then in 1939 Mussolini's Italian troops invaded and annexed the country.

In World War II, after Mussolini was killed, German paratroops occupied Albania, while Communists and Albanian nationalist guerrillas and Greek forces fought the Nazis and each other. At the end of the war, Enver Hoxa, the leader of the Communist resistance, attained power and imposed a bizarre Stalinist and Maoist tyranny that cut the country off from its neighbors and much of the world for more than four decades, leaving it ill prepared for the world after the Cold War.

Growing Tensions

The heart of the tension between Albanians and Serbs became Kosovo. Even there, the conflict was relatively dormant until Milosevic stirred up hostilities in 1989 by revoking the autonomous status that Kosovo had enjoyed in Serbia. Ethnic Albanian Communist leaders were dismissed and a full-scale propaganda campaign was orchestrated by Milosevic against ethnic Albanians, leading to the firing of their teachers and the closing of their schools.

The ethnic Albanian majority of Kosovo then entered into a campaign of passive resistance, setting up its own schools, and a shadow government before the armed resistance, called the Kosovo Liberation Army, which seeks independence for the region, came into full view in 1998.

KOSOVO AT THE CROSSROADS

Tom Hundley

In the following selection, *Chicago Tribune* foreign correspondent
Tom Hundley comments on the ethnic conflict breaking out in
1998 in the Balkan province of Kosovo in the former Yugoslavia.
Hundley writes that tensions among ethnic Albanians and Serbs
have escalated into violence and threaten to intensify. According
to Hundley, Serbs are a small minority in Kosovo, but the province
holds historical significance that makes it very important to their
ethnic identity and sense of nationhood. Many ethnic Albanians,
he says, who make up the large majority of the population of the
province, favor the formation of an independent Kosovo republic.
Although the United Nations and other international organizations are attempting to defuse the situation, Hundley maintains
that the likelihood of a prolonged war over Kosovo is great.

Prizren, a Balkan town of cobblestoned squares and crowded cafes, is
a postcard-pretty place tucked in a deep mountain valley. The center
is a typical blend of Austro-Hungarian and Ottoman architecture. On
the outskirts, white stucco cottages with red tiled roofs creep up the
hillsides.

Signs of apparent normalcy are everywhere: the bustling vegetable
market, the unhurried pace of outdoor diners, the boys playing soccer
in a weed-strewn lot. But just 15 minutes away, similar villages are
being leveled, similar people are seeing their lives turned upside down.

Near a cafe in Prizren's central square stands a 19th Century Serbian Orthodox Church. About 100 yards away is a mosque, even older, built by the Ottoman Turks. It seems almost a certainty that within
a few months, one or the other will be a pile of rubble.

Ethnic Violence Erupts in Kosovo

One Balkan war is ending; another is beginning. Just as the world
is becoming accustomed to the long-standing cease-fire in Bosnia-
Herzegovina, Kosovo is erupting.

Outside the presence of diplomats or journalists, Serb paramilitary
police and regular army units recently shelled ethnic Albanians for

Reprinted from "Kosovo Symbolizes Balkans' Contradiction," by Tom Hundley,
Chicago Tribune, June 10, 1998. Reprinted with permission of Knight Ridder/Tribune
Information Services.

more than a week in the town of Decani and a dozen or so surrounding villages.

According to accounts from fleeing refugees, several villages were reduced to rubble in a routine that became familiar during the war in Bosnia: shell the village until everyone flees, then burn the houses so no one comes back. Of the 65,000 people who lived in the Decani region, relief agencies estimated, more than 40,000 are homeless.

Several thousand have straggled over mountain passes into Albania. Others are hiding in the woods, not more than a few miles from where three American correspondents were enjoying an excellent lunch in Prizren's picturesque central square.

Entry to Pristina Denied

Earlier that morning, we tried to get a firsthand look at the war raging just 10 miles away. We had gotten to within about 3 miles of Djakovica, a village where thousands of ethnic Albanian refugees reportedly were headed, but we were turned back at a Serb police checkpoint.

For three days, we tried to talk our way through Serb checkpoints, but the Serbs were not letting anyone past—not U.S. diplomats, not aid workers and definitely not journalists.

On the first day, we were issued our press credentials at the Serbian government's Secretariat for Information in Pristina, the main city in the unhappy province of Kosovo. One official signaled the way things would be, using a line he obviously had been practicing:

"You can go anywhere you like," said the smirking functionary, "except the places you'd like to go."

Barely beyond the Pristina city limits, the first roadblock was staffed by a half-dozen drunken and surly louts in police uniforms. Fortunately, the one with the Kalashnikov automatic rifle and the mirror sunglasses who seemed to be in charge was sober. The rest of the afternoon was wasted at the local police station.

The first time I came to Pristina was in 1995. The anger, despair and sense of grievance so poisoned the atmosphere that it was one of the few places on Earth I hoped I would never have to see again.

I knew it was wishful thinking.

Kosovo: Serbia's Jerusalem

Kosovo plays a large role in Serb national mythology. It was here in 1389 that Serb warriors were routed by the Ottoman Turks in a spectacularly gory battle. Every Serb school child knows the story. The trauma is endlessly evoked in Serb literature and liturgy and relentlessly exploited by current Serb politicians. The site of the battle is a gently sloping hillside in Kosovo Polje, a few miles from Pristina. "This is our Jerusalem," explained Bozo Spasic, the police chief who prevented us from going anywhere on our first day.

In 1987, on the 598th anniversary of the defeat, Slobodan Milosevic, now the president of Yugoslavia, visited the site and gave a speech. "They will never do this to you again," he told the throng.

Viewed today on videotape, the words by the little-known party functionary hardly seemed dangerous or inspiring. But the moment ignited Milosevic's ascent to political power and marked the beginning of Yugoslavia's descent into the morass of ethnic hatred.

If Kosovo is Serbia's Jerusalem, it also is Serbia's West Bank. Like Israel with its occupation of territory predominantly inhabited by Palestinians, the Serbs face a long-term headache if they want to maintain control of this province. Despite Kosovo's importance to the Serbs' sense of nationhood, very few Serbs live here. Ninety percent of Kosovo's 2.2 million inhabitants are ethnic Albanians.

Serbs vs. Ethnic Albanians

Even in an impoverished region, this is a poor place. Unemployment is more than 40 percent. Only 41 percent of the population is connected to the water system. Even fewer are connected to sewers.

When Yugoslavia was held together by the force of Marshal Tito's will and the co-opting effect of his sharing funds among the federation from the country's coffers, Kosovo was given a remarkable degree of autonomy in an attempt to ease ethnic unrest. Although Albanians were not an officially recognized national group in the old Yugoslav federal system, they were allowed to run their affairs in what amounted to an Albanian mini-state subsidized by Belgrade.

The Serb minority in Kosovo felt besieged and harassed. The Albanians in charge did little to ease their anxieties. Tensions escalated through the 1980s as Albanian nationalists agitated for separation and nervous Serbs began moving out.

In 1990, with Milosevic firmly in control of Serbian politics and ethnic wars about to explode everywhere across Yugoslavia, Belgrade cracked down, stripping Kosovo of its autonomous status and locking Albanian deputies out of their parliament. In response, the lawmakers declared Kosovo an independent and sovereign republic.

The Serbs, in turn, dissolved Kosovo's parliament, silenced the province's Albanian-language television and radio broadcasts, and purged thousands of Albanians from their jobs in the state bureaucracy. Backed by the police and army, it was the Serbs' turn to step on the Albanians.

An End to Non-Violence

Defying Serb rule but not yet embracing armed rebellion, the Albanians moved to establish a parallel, unofficial structure of government, education and health care. The chief architect of this parallel system is Ibrahim Rugova—poet, pacifist and president of the unrecognized Kosovo Republic.

With his trademark scarf, beret and unkempt hair, the professorial

Rugova cuts an unlikely figure among the hard men of the Balkans. His politics of non-violence are a novelty in this region, but for nearly eight years, he has kept a lid on the simmering tensions of Kosovo.

Not for much longer, it seems. Impatient young men, fed up with Rugova's inability to produce anything more substantial than polite applause from the leaders of Europe and the United States, are turning to guns.

As recently as March 1998, there were doubters. Diplomats suspected that the Kosovo Liberation Army, the KLA, was the fabrication of a Serb regime trying to justify ever more repressive measures against the Albanian population. The Albanians did not know whether to believe reports about the existence of a guerrilla group purporting to fight on their behalf.

Events of [May 1998] have resolved most of the doubts. The Serbian police control the main towns and the highways of Kosovo. The KLA effectively controls about one-third of the countryside.

Interview with Gracanica

Just outside Pristina, a few miles from the Kosovo battlefield, we drove up to the gates of the Gracanica monastery, one of the most beautiful of the many medieval monuments that attest to the long and deep attachment of the Serbs to this land. Inside the monastery walls, 15 nuns garbed in black wool habits tend beehives, till fields and pray the prayers of the Serbian Orthodox faith as have their predecessors for centuries.

Pilgrims always are welcome, though not many come these days. A musty gift shop sells votive candles, postcards and souvenir buttons left over from the 600th anniversary of the Kosovo battle.

The monastery predates the battle by about 60 years. It was built by Milutin, one of the greatest Serb kings.

"He was a great warrior but a lousy diplomat. Everything in his time was settled by war," said Snezana Stoyanovic, 26, who works for the provincial government's Institute for the Protection of Historic Monuments. She is curator for the monastery.

Stoyanovic is a heavy-set woman with thick black hair and dark eyes. She is from a small place in central Serbia but moved here to study at the university in Pristina.

She claims she gets along well with her Albanian neighbors in Pristina, although lately, she acknowledged, things have been a little "uncomfortable."

"The Albanians have to understand that this is ours. This is where we have our roots. Everything begins from here," she said. "If anyone tries to take it away, no Serb will allow it."

Many Serbs feel this way—up to a point. The Belgrade press carried a story in the second week of June 1998 about 100 police officers who had been jailed for refusing orders to serve in Kosovo.

Stoyanovic shrugged. "Every day my mother swears at Milosevic. She says she will never send her son to die here. But let me tell you something, she will not be able to stop my brother from coming," she said.

Gracanica is, in the words of Stoyanovic, an "ethnically pure" town. Except for two Albanian families, everyone is Serb. Five small ethnically pure Albanian villages lie on the outskirts of Gracanica.

"We Shall Not Die as Cowards"

In the village of Ajvalija, a huddle of small whitewashed cottages and ragged gardens, people say they feel the war closing in.

"Every day it comes closer. Every day seems like it will be the last day," said Afrim Demaj, a young man in black jeans, a black T-shirt and fashionably short hair. "We have no control over events. All we can do is wait."

Demaj, 24, was a chemistry student at the "parallel" ethnic Albanian university in Pristina, but he quit in frustration after two years because he was never able to conduct a chemistry experiment. He worked as a waiter in Pristina, but he left that job a few weeks ago because the pay was so low it wasn't worth the effort.

His father works as a forklift operator in Switzerland and sends money to support the family.

"My father's dream was to go to Switzerland, save some money, and come back here and build something. But now we need him there more than here. We need money to buy weapons."

I asked if he or any of the other young men in Ajvalija had weapons. He said no.

"I see these KLA people who have started to fight, and my feeling is that this is not the way to solve our problem. But it seems it is the only way left to us," he said.

Did that mean that if his village came under threat, would he join the KLA?

"We shall not die as cowards. I promise you that," he said quietly.

Macedonia Is the Key

That there will be a wider war in Kosovo is, by now, pretty much a foregone conclusion. The guns are everywhere. You can buy a Kalashnikov in the Pristina greenmarket for 200 German marks, about $120. One diplomat told us that the Serb authorities were handing out grenade launchers to civilians. Another diplomat confirmed it.

This is exactly the way it began in Bosnia.

The big concern in European capitals and Washington is not how to stop the fighting in Kosovo but how to contain it, how to prevent it from sloshing over the borders and igniting a much larger Balkan conflict. NATO is considering the possibility of putting troops on the borders in Albania and Macedonia.

Macedonia is the key. There are 350 American troops in this land-locked Balkan state, part of a UN peacekeeping mission that was placed along the Serbian border in 1992.

Macedonia straddles the fault line of every Balkan war fought during the last 150 years. In a worst-case scenario, a conflict there could spread to Greece, Turkey, Bulgaria and Yugoslavia. Greece and Turkey, two NATO members, would be on opposing sides.

Albania is less important in the West's calculus. The central government's authority does not extend beyond the capital, Tirana. The army is non-functional. The mountainous territory along the Kosovo border is controlled by bandits, smugglers and warlords.

In addition, Albanians who live in Albania have little in common with their Kosovo cousins except a language and a set of traditions.

Kosovo Albanians and the Albanians of Macedonia, on the other hand, are one and the same people. For 73 years, they lived together as citizens of the same country, Yugoslavia. They went to the same schools. They frequently intermarried, and their kinship ties are extensive. Now they are separated by a 7-year-old border that, to them, is a meaningless nuisance.

Ethnic Albanians Want More Rights

Since we seemed to be making no progress at the Serb checkpoints, we packed up the Jeep and headed for Skopje, the Macedonian capital.

Ethnic Albanians make up about 23 percent of Macedonia's population. They are pushing for more rights and greater autonomy against a fair degree of Macedonian chauvinism. But the situation is not nearly so bad as it is in Kosovo.

At least in Macedonia, the two sides are talking to each other. There are Albanian parties in the governing coalition as well as in the opposition.

On short notice, we were granted an interview with Kiro Gligorov, the 81-year-old president of Macedonia and one of the great Balkan survivors. Two years ago, he survived a car bomb attack that took out an eye and a large section of his skull.

In his large but somewhat threadbare office, Gligorov related a conversation he had in the fall of 1998 with Milosevic in which the Serbian leader told him, "We have a common enemy and we should fight the Albanians together."

Gligorov said he declined the offer. "I was very persistent that we could not follow the example they were setting in Kosovo."

One of the Skopje government's sharpest critics is Arben Xhaferi, 50, leader of the Democratic Party of Albanians.

On the afternoon that we dropped by Xhaferi's office in Tetevo, a predominantly Albanian city in western Macedonia, he apologized for being unable to stifle his yawns.

He explained that he had been up until 6 a.m. watching Game 2 of the Bulls–Utah Jazz series.

Xhaferi said he thinks the war in Kosovo inevitably will spill into Macedonia with unpredictable consequences. He suggested we drive to the border and have a look for ourselves.

At the Border

Too insignificant to appear on most maps, Jazince is a village of almost surreal beauty set in the foothills of mountains that rise to snowy peaks. The first thing I noticed was that ours was the only car in the village. The second thing was the KLA graffiti on the walls.

The men in Jazince are reluctant to talk about it. When we cautiously brought up the subject in the village's only cafe, everyone stopped talking. Heads swung around toward our table.

"They don't exist here," said Idriz Bajrami, 63. Then, after a moment, he added: "We are all KLA if we are needed."

The men brought us out to the border, which actually cuts through the property of the last house in the village.

Serb authorities claim their border patrols have had clashes with gun smugglers in these mountains. The men of Jazince only shrugged.

Lt. Col. Lauri Ovaska, a Finn who commands the UN peacekeepers responsible for this sector, says there have been no clashes. He also says there is a lot of cross-border smuggling but that it is mostly cigarettes and drugs, not guns. The sector under Ovaska's control includes a roughly 60-mile stretch of mountains with more than 20 peaks more than a mile high.

"Nobody can seal that kind of area, if by seal you mean that if somebody is crossing, he will be killed. It would take half a million soldiers to do that," he said.

A Never-Ending War

We get word that the shelling has stopped and, under international pressure, the Serbs are allowing some reporters and diplomats into the Decani area. Dispatches said the scene recalled some of the worst destruction in Bosnia, describing houses gutted by fire and stray livestock roaming deserted villages.

My own hunch is that the fighting in Kosovo will not be another Bosnia. Another conflict comes to mind: the never-ending war between Turkey and its Kurdish minority.

Serbia, with its superior firepower and Soviet-era military doctrine, will try to crush the KLA by leveling villages. The KLA will mount guerrilla raids, then retreat across the border into the mountain fastness of Albania and Macedonia. Neither side has the strength to defeat the other outright. This looks like it could be a long war.

CHAPTER 5

ETHNIC VIOLENCE IN AFRICA AND ASIA

Contemporary Issues
Companion

THE BLOODY HISTORY OF HUTU-TUTSI RELATIONS

Leo J. DeSouza

In the following selection, Leo J. DeSouza explores the long legacy of conflict between the Hutu and the Tutsi, two ethnic groups
who live in Rwanda and Burundi. In 1994, DeSouza explains, the
Hutu of Rwanda massacred hundreds of thousands of Rwandan
Tutsi. While the international outrage against the Hutu for the
slaughter is understandable, he writes, the Tutsi are not completely innocent victims. The Tutsi have a long history of oppressing
and killing the Hutu, DeSouza claims, and he warns that many
Tutsi may now seek violent revenge for the 1994 massacre. In his
view, understanding the history of the relationship between the
two groups can help to end the cycle of violence in Rwanda. De-
Souza calls for a general amnesty for all combatants except the
highest Hutu leaders and an investigation by an impartial organization such as the Organization of African Unity or the United
Nations. DeSouza worked as an orthopedic surgeon consultant in
Uganda. He now practices medicine in Minneapolis and teaches
at the medical school of the University of Minnesota.

On September 26, 1996, the United Nations's International Criminal
Tribunal for Rwanda began genocide trials in Arusha, a small town at
the foot of Mt. Kilimanjaro in Tanzania. The man in the dock was
Jean-Paul Akayesu, former mayor of Taba in Rwanda and the first
Hutu to be tried by the Tribunal. He is accused of atrocities in his district, where 2,000 Tutsi lie buried in two mass graves after being
hacked to death with machetes.

Akayesu pleaded not guilty and asked for postponement, but when
the trial resumed in January 1997, the international community
renewed its cry for justice, i.e, for the blood of the Hutu.

Certainly, the public outrage is understandable. The story of the
majority Hutu population's massacre of Rwanda's Tutsi minority is
one of unimaginable viciousness and violence. The events immediately preceding the massacre and the subsequent months prior to the

overthrow of the government by Tutsi rebels are familiar to—and abhorred by—most readers: On April 6, 1994, Rwandan President Juvenal Habyarimana was returning from a peace conference in Tanzania. Also aboard his plane was Cyprien Ntaryamira, president of neighboring Burundi. Both were members of the region's majority Hutu tribe. Preparing to land on the palace grounds, the plane was shot down, killing both men.

Reaction was instantaneous. Within hours the Rwandan Presidential Guard (dominated by Hutu) went on a rampage, killing Rwanda's Tutsi Prime Minister and other members of the opposition party sympathetic to the Tutsi. Soldiers and militiamen joined in. They fanned out across the city looking for Tutsi.

The slaughter had begun.

The Spread of Killings

From Kigali the killing spread to towns, prefectural capitals, and hillside settlements. Across the country, the Tutsi were massacred in their homes, in open fields, along broad roads, and even as they hid in the bushes. They were slain with stones and axes, machetes and clubs, hand grenades and guns.

In a Roman Catholic church, an orange brick building in the town square of one village, 1,200 Tutsi sought refuge. The local Hutu mayor had promised police protection. But the following morning, soldiers appeared, blew open the locked church door with a hand grenade, and fired into the huddled mass. They returned the next morning to finish off those who had survived, leaving only bodies, blood, and silence.

In another "safe" church, a Hutu mob swarmed in, hacking and clubbing frightened women and children to death. Tutsi patients disappeared from hospitals; Tutsi students from schools. Tutsi teenage girls were raped. Hutu mothers with babies strapped to their backs killed Tutsi mothers with babies strapped to their backs; Hutu 10-year-olds killed Tutsi 10-year-olds. Before it was over, half a million Rwandans were dead. They were almost all Tutsi, along with a few Hutu who had refused to go along with the carnage.

As the Tutsi were being decimated in Rwanda, Tutsi exiles living in Uganda felt the time for action was at hand. Calling themselves the "Rwandan Patriotic Front," the rebels entered the country from the north and advanced swiftly toward the capital. They had had a running battle with the Hutu ever since the country gained independence in 1962 and democratic elections had put the more numerous Hutu in power. Now, pushing with the ferocity of the dispossessed, the exiled Tutsi overran the country and by July 18, 1994, had taken over the capital and declared victory.

The victorious Tutsi quickly ascertained that the violence that had seized the country since the president's crash was not the result of random acts. They determined that the killings had been organized, encouraged, even ordered by the Hutu government officials at the highest level, whose intent had been to wipe out the Tutsi from Rwanda. Within two weeks, the Tutsi government announced that they would "proceed with war-crimes trials of . . . the ousted government and . . . civilians suspected of taking part in the genocidal attacks." In December 1994, the UN created the International War-Crimes Tribunal for Rwanda, with trials to be held in the neutral territory of Tanzania. Some 400 Hutu were to be charged with planning and organizing the massacres.

To those following the conflict on the evening news, the Hutu-Tutsi conflict seems entirely straightforward, if somewhat incredible. Comparisons to the Nazi extermination of the Jews have been tossed around. But the Rwanda conflict, while tragic, is considerably more complicated. The Tutsi of Central Africa are not quite the peace-loving victims of Western imagination. Over the years, they have committed a long list of atrocities of their own. The international community's ignorance of this history has caused them to treat the Tutsi who now rule Rwanda as noble victims—and to ignore the danger that the Tutsi will use their newfound power to exact bloody revenge on the Hutu. And if that happens, the cycle of genocidal violence in Rwanda will only continue. (Already, in Eastern Congo, Tutsi are believed to be exterminating the fleeing Hutu refugees.) The only hope of ending that cycle lies in understanding the full history of Hutu-Tutsi relations and adopting an approach which takes that history into account.

A Centuries-Old Grudge

The Hutu's fear and hatred of the Tutsi has its roots in centuries of abuse. The Hutu were in Rwanda long before anyone, other than the Bantu tribes. The Tutsi arrived much later, around the 15th century, from the northeast. Theirs was a slow and peaceful infiltration. But over time they used their cattle and their warring skills to build their power and prestige. Whenever the Hutu needed the use of cattle, they worked for the Tutsi owner as payment. This simple arrangement eventually crystallized into a feudal-type class system. Land, cattle, and power were consolidated in the hands of the Tutsi, and the Hutu became serfs. Hutu peasants bound themselves to individual Tutsi lords, giving land, produce, and personal services in exchange for the lord's protection and use of his cattle. Tall and aristocratic in bearing, the Tutsi claimed they were divinely ordained to rule. In this manner, the Tutsi minority—between 10 and 20 percent of the population— held dominion over the Hutu for 400 years.

In 1885 Europe's colonial powers convened at a conference in Berlin to carve up the African continent. Rwanda was pronounced a German colony. The Germans ruled Rwanda through the Tutsi king, or Mwami, who, in turn, used German forces to strengthen his own position.

Since the Europeans governed their colonies ostensibly to enlighten poor backward souls and to introduce them to the concept of fairness, one would have thought that the Europeans would have attempted to relieve the Hutu from serfdom. Far from it. What little flexibility had previously existed between the Tutsi lords and the Hutu vanished during the colonial era. It was during this period that the Mwami came closer to absolute rule than at any other time. Hutu rebellion was dealt with swiftly: Villages were burnt and leaders executed—with guns supplied by Europeans. It was no different when the Belgians took over during World War I. From 1916 until Rwandan independence in 1962, the Belgians ruled through the Tutsi aristocracy.

The Europeans were always attracted to the Tutsi. Unlike the Hutu, who are a dark people, short and squat, with coarse features, the Tutsi are tall and fair, with finer features that reminded Europeans of themselves. The Germans and Belgians romanticized the tall Tutsi as Africa's elite. Schools were open to them and admission to college was fixed in their favor, by requiring applicants to pass a minimum height test. They were assured of the best jobs.

This modus operandi was not unusual among colonial rulers. They often selected an elite minority group to help administer their far-flung colonies. It was a way of creating a client community, a tactic that divided the colonized population while consolidating colonial rule. In Lebanon, the Maronites were the anointed ones; in Egypt, the Copts; and in northern India, the Sikhs. In Rwanda, the system was even more flagrant: It consolidated the higher status of the Tutsi by emphasizing the differences between them and the Hutu. The Belgians even introduced identity cards, requiring everyone to be recognized by their tribe.

In the years leading up to Rwanda's independence, the country's High Council, a Tutsi body, called for urgent training of the Tutsi elite in preparation for self-government—a plain attempt to perpetuate Tutsi dominance. The Hutu leaders countered with "The Manifesto of the Bahutu" which sought to end the Tutsi's stranglehold on the government. The Belgians ignored the manifesto; the Tutsi spurned it. One Tutsi group said: "Relations between us and them have forever been based on servitude; therefore, there is no feeling of fraternity whatsoever between them and us. . . . Since our Kings have conquered all of the Hutu's lands by killing their monarchs and enslaving their people, how can they now pretend to be our brothers?" Tensions mounted in 1959. In a last ditch attempt to hold onto power, the Tutsi began massacring any Hutu they believed might stand in their way. Francois Karera, a senior politician in the former Hutu government, now an exile in eastern Congo, was a young teacher in 1959 when the Hutu rose up for the first time. He recalls that period as one when he, as an educated Hutu, was "hunted" by Tutsi for daring to aspire to a higher standing than a mere peasant farmer. But the Hutu prevailed. In the sporadic violence of that period, more than 20,000 Tutsi were displaced. In 1962, Rwanda became independent and held national elections. The Hutu candidate Kayibanda was elected President following a Hutu victory at the polls.

This did not sit well with the Tutsi. Their militants organized into guerrilla bands, and casualties escalated. Between 1961 and 1966, the Inyenzi, or cockroaches, as the Tutsi militants called themselves, launched 10 major attacks from neighboring countries—Uganda, Tanzania, Burundi, and Zaire. The rebellions prompted severe retaliation from the Hutu in power. In 1963, about 10,000 Tutsi were killed following an Inyenzi attack from Burundi. Eventually defeated, they fell back into exile. Tutsi refugees totaled 150,000. The story repeated itself in 1973 when more Tutsi were killed on suspicion of their involvement in a coup in which the Hutu General Habyarimana deposed Rwanda's first President. (Habyarimana subsequently died in the fateful 1994 plane crash that triggered the latest round of violence.)

Massacres in Burundi

Events in neighboring Burundi served to further inflame the Hutu-Tutsi hatreds in Rwanda. Rwanda and Burundi are practically replicas of one another. Alike in size and population, they have the same tribal mix of Hutu and Tutsi, share much of the same history, and were part of the same colony.

Like Rwanda, Burundi became independent in 1962. But unlike Rwanda, Burundi's Tutsi minority has retained power and, to this day, rules the country. In the late '60s and early '70s, when the Tutsi in Burundi began to fear that the country's more numerous Hutu would come to power as they had in Rwanda, the Tutsi came up with a simple solution: eliminate the Hutu in Burundi. In 1972, they set out to massacre every Hutu with an education, a government job, or money. Within three months 250,000 Hutu were dead, their homes destroyed.

"Many Hutu were taken from their homes at night," wrote David Lamb of the *Los Angeles Times* in his book *The Africans*. "Others received summonses to report to the police station. So obedient, subservient, and hopeless had the Hutus become that they answered the summons, which even the most unlearned soul knew was really an execution notice. Sometimes, when the death quotas at the prisons and police stations had been filled for the day, the queued-up Hutu were told to return the next day. They dutifully complied. The few Hutu who tried to escape the executioners seemed to make only token attempts. It was a pathetic sight. They would walk down the main road toward the border. If the Tutsi gendarme stopped them," he continued, "they would turn quietly back."

A quarter of a million Hutu were slain in three months, but the world did not take notice. Nobody called it genocide, then or now.

And nobody asked that the Tutsi in Burundi be tried. (To this day, sporadic killing of the Hutu continues in Burundi, and recently there has been an ominous escalation.)

What Next?

Meanwhile, for lack of funds and assistance, Rwanda's unsuccessful Tutsi rebels lived quietly in exile until October of 1990. At that time, using Uganda as a base, the Rwandan Patriotic Front launched an invasion. Their stated aim: to take over the government in order to protect the Tutsi. By then, they had regrouped, retrained, and re-armed with new and heavier weapons. The initial assault was repelled by the Hutu government, but skirmishes continued through 1991 and 1992. A cease-fire was called in January 1993, but the Tutsi attacked again. On August 4, 1993, a peace agreement was signed in Tanzania. Implementation of the agreement, however, was slow. And when Rwanda's Hutu President was killed in April of 1994, there was wide-spread fear among the Hutu that another Tutsi rebellion was again underway. "In the Hutu mind, the Tutsi were going to bring back their regime; we the Hutu were going to work for them again, and the educated Hutu would be killed as in 1959," says François Karera, who insists the Hutu's subsequent massacre of the Tutsi was driven by fear and self-preservation. "The Hutu were determined," claims Karera, "not to allow the Tutsi to repeat history."

In contrast to the indifference with which the international com-munity greeted the 1972 massacre of Hutu in Burundi, the 1994 mas-sacre of Tutsi in Rwanda provoked global outrage. Television photog-raphers and newspaper reporters told the tragedy as it unfolded, without reference to events in Burundi or what had previously tran-spired in Rwanda. The whole world judged the Hutu crimes as an iso-lated act.

Now that they are back in power, the Tutsi of Rwanda have embarked on their own broad investigation and prosecution of Hutu genocidaires. In contrast to the international tribunal in Tanzania, which is focused on the leaders of the massacre, the Rwandan govern-ment's probe is centered on lower-level civilians. Early reports are troubling. In the first week of 1997, a Rwandan court at Kibungo sen-tenced two Hutu men to death after a four-hour trial. More trials have now begun in Kigali and Byumba. The prisons in Rwanda are current-ly packed with 85,000 Hutu. A facility built to hold 500 inmates now holds 7,000. Prisoners cannot sit or lie down for lack of space. So they stand, four to a square yard, in the muddy central courtyard. It takes hours to reach the latrines or the cooking fires. For 7,000 people there are 21 latrines, 5 of them designated for dysentery sufferers who try to stay nearby. There is no protection against heavy rain and many pris-oners' feet show signs of rotting from gangrene. A few die every day. "It is horrific," said Dr. Alison Davis, of the relief agency Doctors

Without Borders. "They are being treated like animals. It is true that some or many may have been involved in the killing, but the way they are treated is not justice."

Whatever their motivation—fear or simple hatred—the Hutu should, of course, be held accountable for their slaughter of the Tutsi. But while it's advisable to punish the Hutu leaders who incited the population to commit the atrocities, it is a grave mistake to go after the low-level perpetrators. True, many crimes would go unpunished. But this is a situation where achieving justice at the level of individual cases is less important than putting a stop to the endless cycle of violence. If, with the acquiescence of the international community, the Tutsi government continues to prosecute low-level Hutus without also holding local Tutsis responsible for their past deeds, the Hutu of Rwanda will feel justified in taking their counter-revenge the next time they're on top. The only way to end the bloodletting in Rwanda once and for all is to declare a general amnesty for all but the highest level perpetrators and establish a truth commission similar to the one in South Africa, charged with investigating the fate of victims on both sides even as it forgives most of their attackers. This could initially be conducted under the aegis of the Organization of African Unity, or the UN, or both. But unless it is done, another genocide is waiting to happen: The Tutsi will kill the Hutu, and then, of course, the Hutu will kill the Tutsi.

ACHIEVING JUSTICE AND ETHNIC RECONCILIATION IN RWANDA

Samantha Power

In 1994 in Rwanda, hundreds of thousands of Tutsis were systematically massacred by another Rwandan ethnic group, the
Hutu. In the following selection, Samantha Power describes the
situation in Rwanda four years after the 1994 massacre. Those
Hutus who are still in prison awaiting trial, sentencing, or execution show no remorse for the genocide they perpetrated on the
Tutsis, Power claims. However, she writes that hope for the country exists in the form of the new Tutsi-led government, which
she credits with trying to institute positive change in spite of
being faced with such difficulties as a lack of resources, a failing
judicial and legal system, and the distrust displayed by the
Hutus. Power believes that what happens to Rwanda in the long
run hinges on the discipline and idealism of the Tutsi-led government. Power is an author and an advisor to the International
Crisis Group, a multinational organization headquartered in
Brussels, Belgium.

From a distance the Gitarama prison's outer walls appear to shimmer.
It's an optical illusion created by hundreds of thin, sweaty arms pok-
ing in and out of narrow slits in the prison's facade. The Gitarama
inmates are pleading for water from a guard dozing in the nearby
shade, but he ignores them. During the spring of 1995, nine Rwandans per day died in this jail. Conditions have improved, but dehy-
dration, disease, and suffocation remain common. Across the country,
about 120,000 genocide suspects are locked up in similar conditions.
Some have been imprisoned without cause, many without formal
charges, and nearly all without hope of trial, let alone release, any
time in the next decade. And the arrests continue, thanks in part to
local thugs who, in their eagerness to get their hands on the land and
cows of their neighbors, will pay $33 plus a cut of the loot to anyone
willing to denounce one of his countrymen as a genocidaire.

The Rwandan government is attempting to apply a legal solution

Reprinted from "Life After Death," Samantha Power, *New Republic,* April 6, 1998, by
permission of *The New Republic.* Copyright ©1998, The New Republic, Inc.

to a most monstrous crime—the Hutu militants' cold-blooded massacre of 800,000 Tutsi and moderate Hutu during a 100-day frenzy in
1994. But so far the Tutsi-dominated government's one-year-old judicial experiment is satisfying no one.

There are so many cases to be tried that, at the current pace, 97 percent of Gitarama's inmates will probably die of old age before they
ever see a courtroom. And of those "lucky" enough to face a judge,
only half will have lawyers, usually Belgian or West African counsel
supplied by Avocats sans Frontieres, or Lawyers without Borders—an
organization initially scorned by survivors as "Genocidaires sans
Frontieres." The accused get no more than three days to examine
their case files, and witnesses rarely testify for fear of instant denunci-
ation or retaliation. In the nearly 350 trials conducted as of early
1998, a little over one-third of the suspects have been sentenced to
death. None of these sentences has been carried out yet. But survivors
of the genocide are getting restive, and the executions are expected to
commence in the coming months.

Philbert Sindayiga is one of those calling for an eye for an eye. A
25-year-old Tutsi farmer, Sindayiga lost his father, four sisters, and
three brothers in the onslaught of 1994. I met him in a church in the
town of Nyamata, where he now spends his days in the morbid company of the skulls and bones of his murdered relatives. His family's
remains are on display there amid those of some 25,000 Rwandans
who had vainly sought shelter in the church and surrounding hills.
Sindayiga beckons me to a corner where he and a friend pull the blan-
ket off a musty bundle to reveal the lime-green corpse of a murdered
Tutsi woman whom they have managed to preserve with a local
chemical brew. "The killers must be punished, or else we will be
forced to take justice into our own hands," he explains, covering the
grisly monument. "And, if we do that, there'll be no difference
between us and them."

A Tutsi-Led Government Takes Over

Indeed, after the current Tutsi-led government defeated the Hutu
regime in August 1994, it made a concerted effort to distinguish itself
from its genocidal predecessor. It was an almost unprecedented
instance of victims snatching power from their victimizers, and the
early gestures were impressive. The new government placed members
of the majority Hutu (who make up 85 percent of the population) in
the senior ranks of its ministries, urged Hutu refugees to return home,
and preached tolerance, coexistence, and respect for human rights. As
one prominent member of parliament put it, "We did not come here
only to take power. We came here to change things in this country."

Given that as many as 100,000 Hutu had just taken part in a killing
spree that wiped out nearly half of Rwanda's Tutsi populace, international observers found the new government's stance admirable. But in

1998, as the regime struggles to quell a Hutu rebellion that aims to finish the job of 1994, the international community is bitterly divided over whether the Rwandan government has abandoned its stated ideals. On one side of this vitriolic debate are human rights groups that insist the gap between the old regime and the new is narrowing. They note that, though far from genocidal, the current government has locked up tens of thousands of Hutu without explanation, harassed its political opponents, and expressed little public remorse about massacring civilians while ferreting out Hutu rebels. When Hutu insurgents strike Tutsi soldiers or civilians, the Tutsi-led army usually responds in kind and often in excess—unintentionally earning the Hutu militants new recruits in the process. The army has warned that anyone who shelters or even sympathizes with Hutu rebels may be arrested or attacked. In 1997, according to U.N. monitors, government forces murdered at least 8,000 Hutu. And, during the spring of 1998, soldiers have been engaged in a violent "mop up" operation, killing several hundred Hutu in retaliation for a recent Hutu assault that left 19 Tutsi dead. Thus, it's not altogether surprising that nearly half of the Hutu genocide suspects who have escaped from prison have turned themselves back in, reasoning that they are safer inside the overcrowded jails than outside.

But, while human rights watchdogs cry foul, American and European governments take the opposite stance—keeping largely mum over these abuses, emphasizing the unparalleled obstacles the Tutsi regime must overcome, and pumping in aid to help them do so. . . .

The major powers choose to continue their support for the current regime partly because they are guilt-ridden over having failed to halt the 1994 genocide. (France has even launched a parliamentary investigation into its role in arming the Hutu attackers.) But they also believe that this underresourced and overwhelmed government deserves the benefit of the doubt. They feel, with good reason, that it would be incorrect and immoral to analyze the state policy in isolation. After all, the Hutu militants managed to murder more people more quickly than any other regime in the modern era. Furthermore, while today's prison conditions and judicial deviances are deplorable, this is largely due to the decimated state of Rwanda's legal system. Even before the genocide, fewer than half of Rwanda's judges and magistrates had received any formal legal training. During the slaughter, most judges, prosecutors, and criminal investigators either became killers or cadavers. By the fall of 1994, only 244 judges, 14 prosecutors, and 39 investigators remained to tackle close to a million homicides.

Hutu Jail Breaks and Massacres

Meanwhile, far from ceasing their murderous mischief, Hutu genocidaires are still on the loose. Initially, when the Hutu regime was first defeated, some two million Hutu (an unwieldy mix of militant masterminds, blood-stained foot soldiers, and terrified bystanders) fled to neighboring countries. But, over the course of 1996, the refugee camps were closed (many forcibly), and more than one-and-a-half million Hutu refugees opted to take their chances and go back to Rwanda. Upon their return, many were registered and then either arrested on genocide charges or whisked off to "solidarity camps" so they could be "reoriented" (some say brainwashed) to sympathize with their new governors. The ringleaders of the genocide knew enough to stay away, but 23 of them—including the former Hutu prime minister and defense minister—were later nabbed in Africa and Europe and extradited to the International War Crimes Tribunal in neighboring Tanzania, where they will be tried. They will receive a maximum of life imprisonment (probably somewhere in Scandinavia), while the most serious "Category One" culprits processed in the Rwandan system (in most cases somewhat smaller fry) will get death.

But many killers have slipped through the cracks. December 1997 and January 1998 were the bloodiest months since 1994, as an increasingly sophisticated network of Hutu rebel bands orchestrated jailbreaks that freed more than 1,000 Hutu prisoners as well as massacres that targeted the most vulnerable Tutsi civilians—women and children living in refugee camps.

The Hard Road to National Reconciliation

International donors and leading states decided early on to throw their weight and money behind the legal remedy, spending $18 million on judicial infrastructure and training in a country where half of the population lives on less than a dollar per day. But the money can only achieve so much. Fifteen miles down the road from the Gitarama prison, for example, the European Union is funding a five-month training camp for police investigators. When I visited, 150 sprightly trainees were just filing into their plush new home, which is decked with palm trees, flower beds, cobbled pathways, and a fullsize football field. These newcomers had no experience, but they just passed a 14-question entrance exam, and, upon earning their badges, whistles, and motorbikes, they will be dispatched to investigate the crimes of 1994 in the hopes of expediting the trial process. They are, in essence, genocide cops. And, since only a few dozen investigators remained in Rwanda after the genocide, the Belgian who administered the test couldn't afford to be too discriminating. Most of those accepted in the program identified cannabis—not as (a) a variety of sugar cane, (b) a drug extracted from hemp, or (c) a soft drink—but as (d) a predatory bird. The well-meaning training camp may be creating Rwanda's law enforcers of the future, but there is simply no way that the planned 500-investigator force will be able to process the monumental sins of the past.

And, as daunting as the logistical hurdles to national reconciliation may be, they are nothing compared to the psychological ones. Generally speaking, since the Hutu responsible for the genocide believe they did their people a service (exterminating the *inyenzi*, or "cockroaches," as they call the Tutsi), they are not sorry. Euphrasie Kamatamu is an alleged Category One killer. Accused of plotting massacres, selling forged Hutu identity cards to Tutsi women and girls, and then steering machete-wielders their way, she has been placed in the elite class of "instigators," "sexual torturers," or "notorious murderers," who "distinguished themselves" by exhibiting excessive zeal or malice in carrying out the crimes. If convicted, she will automatically be sentenced to death. Yet the plump, shaved-headed Kamatamu, who is being tried jointly along with her husband and two military escorts, appears undaunted. She saunters into the Kigali courtroom, caresses the crucifix around her neck, and smiles at her hostile neighbors who line the aisles. Like virtually all genocide suspects in custody—including the 23 being held by the United Nations in Tanzania—she steps up to the bench and pleads "not guilty."

Plagued as it is by remorseless killers, keystone cops, and bursting prisons, the legal remedy looks most unpromising. Which is what one might expect four years after a genocide of such scale. Unfortunately, and perhaps unjustly, Rwanda's long-term future depends less on the international community (which will go on giving) or the Hutu genocidaires (who will go on killing) but on the discipline, and even idealism, of the Tutsi-led government. Neither Rwanda's borders nor its citizens will ever be secure until the state can enshrine the rule of law, respect the rights of all, and someday create a pluralistic political landscape. But, to get there, the Tutsi regime will have to recommit itself to doing more than merely distinguishing itself from an utterly ignoble predecessor.

A Threat of Genocide in Burundi

Bruce W. Nelan

In 1994, thousands of Hutus fleeing the ethnic killing in their African homeland of Rwanda sought refuge in the neighboring country of Burundi, which has a large Hutu population. In the following selection, Bruce W. Nelan, a foreign correspondent for Time-Life News Services, explains that the Rwandan Hutu have not found a safe haven in Burundi, where they have become targets of violence perpetrated by their ethnic rivals, the Tutsi. Nelan writes that bands of Tutsi militiamen seeking revenge for the 1994 genocide in Rwanda have taken over the Burundi capital of Bujumbura, killing or driving out Hutu residents. Furthermore, he notes that the Hutu and Tutsi people of Burundi also have a long history of ethnic conflict, which could be reignited by the ethnic violence spilling over from Rwanda. Burundian and foreign officials alike are alarmed by this situation and are concerned that the genocide that decimated Rwanda will be repeated in Burundi, Nelan reports.

The spectacle was sickeningly familiar. Thousands of refugees, most of them Rwandan Hutu, clogged the rutted roads of central Africa last week [the first week of April 1995]. Thousands of men, women and children were on the move in Burundi, fleeing camps where they had sought asylum last year from the civil war in their homeland next door. Now, spurred by the dread of more ethnic killing, they trudged east toward Tanzania. As they passed other Hutu camps, more thousands gathered up their meager belongings to join the trek. About 40,000 refugees were stalled Saturday just outside Tanzania after the country closed its borders.

For months, sporadic tribal killing has been fracturing Burundi into tense ethnic cantonments, which many officials in the country and outside fear could explode into full-scale genocide. Fresh and ominous spasms of bloodshed erupted in the capital as well as the Majuri refugee camp near the town of Ngozi, where armed men killed 12 Rwandan Hutu and wounded 22 last Monday. That attack, presumably carried out by Tutsi militiamen, followed a week of ethnic cleans-

Reprinted, with permission, from "A Recurring Nightmare," by Bruce W. Nelan, *Time*, April 10, 1995. Copyright ©1995 Time Inc.

ing in the capital, Bujumbura: bands of Tutsi swept through mixed neighborhoods, driving out members of the other tribal group, fighting with Hutu militia, shooting stragglers, burning houses and shops. Families were shot in the street and left to die; mothers came home to murdered children.

"Youths came with guns and took everything," says Ahmed Brown, a Hutu whose left eye is swollen from a blow with a club. He is still living in his old neighborhood but says, "I am so afraid. We have seen too many people gunned down." Bujumbura is now mainly Tutsi, its Hutu residents forced into a few ghettolike areas like the northern section of the city called Kamenge. Out in the countryside, Hutu gangs roam the hills around Tutsi encampments, preying on those who venture out.

Rumors spread quickly last week that the Tutsi-dominated army was about to attack Kamenge and seven major refugee camps that provide shelter to 200,000 Hutu from Rwanda. Tutsi paramilitary groups may have spread the rumors themselves to help speed their segregation plan. Everyone in Burundi is still in shock after the massacres in Rwanda [in 1994], in which more than 500,000 Rwandans, mostly Tutsi, were slaughtered.

The latest outbreak of communal violence was touched off by a pair of assassinations [in March 1995] that have put extremists into power on both sides. First a Hutu government minister, a respected moderate, was shot and killed. A few days later Hutu vigilantes took their revenge by kidnapping a moderate Tutsi politician, a former mayor of Bujumbura. His body was found crucified and eviscerated.

Officials in Burundi and the world outside have been watching anxiously to see if the Rwandan nightmare would repeat itself here. The ethnic makeup in Burundi is the same as in Rawanda: 80% Hutu, 15% Tutsi. The difference is that in Burundi, the minority Tutsi have always controlled the armed forces, while in Rwanda the majority had the weapons. After the assassination of two presidents in 18 months, the current government is a shaky coalition of the two rival tribal groups. Moderates willing to compromise are dumped by their own faction, and, says a senior foreign-aid worker, "the country has been taken hostage by the hard-liners."

In an interview with *Time* last week, President Sylvestre Ntibantunganya, a Hutu, vowed to prevent more killing by disarming the Hutu and Tutsi militias, but conceded that extremist vigilantes had official sponsors on both sides. "These militias are not created out of thin air," he said. "They are essentially political, and there are politicians who fund and direct them." Diplomats doubted whether the Burundi government, which survives on sufferance of the two factions and is reshuffled regularly, would be able to disarm anyone.

Outsiders have been trying to keep the lid on mainly by reminding the government that the rest of the world is watching. Humanitarian assistance has been arriving steadily—including $77 million from the U.S. since October 1993—and so have high-level visitors like Deputy Secretary of State Strobe Talbott. The U.N. has assigned a special representative to Burundi to help keep the governing coalition in place. Last week the Security Council warned that it would consider taking "appropriate measures to bring to justice" those who commit genocide.

Though there was much hand wringing last year about the world's failure to stop the slaughter in Rwanda, intervention seems no more likely this time. The U.S. and other members of the Security Council have turned down Secretary-General Boutros Boutros-Ghali's proposal for a rapid-deployment force to be placed on call in Zaire. "That's crazy," says a Washington official. "No country is willing or able to put troops there."

U.S. officials describe themselves as "pessimistic but not defeatist." Though violence is widespread, they say they hope it can be contained. They argue that genocide took place in Rwanda, where the Hutu were in full control, but in Burundi there is a rough balance of power: the Hutu have the numbers and the Tutsi the guns. Diplomats in Bujumbura tend to agree. "It's not genocide," says one. "It's a slow-burn civil war."

LOST IN THE HELL OF WAR

Tony Clifton

For several decades, the island nation of Sri Lanka has been the scene of a violent ethnic conflict between the minority Tamils, who are mostly Hindu, and the majority Sinhalese, who are primarily Buddhist. The Tamils want to establish an autonomous homeland in the eastern and northern provinces of Sri Lanka, but the Sinhalese are strongly opposed to this idea. In the following selection, Tony Clifton describes the devastating effect the Tamil-Sinhalese conflict has had on Sri Lanka. According to Clifton, more than 80,000 Sri Lankans have been killed or have disappeared in a war of attrition that is robbing the country of its young men. In addition, he writes, war costs have stunted the economy of this nation, which otherwise has the potential to become one of the wealthiest in the region. Clifton reports on the news in Asia for *Newsweek International*.

The European tourists have flocked to Sri Lanka again this year, and, as always, the country's endless guerrilla war seems so far away. The occasional military roadblock aside, there's nothing to stop the fun in Colombo. The MGM Grand and other casinos are humming, the Hilton's Blue Elephant disco is hopping and elegant restaurants like the Paradise Road Galerie are filled with diners who think nothing of spending the equivalent of a soldier's monthly pay on dinner for two. The southern beaches at Bentota and Galle are packed with bathers, awash in beer. Beach boys circulate everywhere, making their offers in German or English: "Smoke? Girl? Or you want boy?" Yes, that's what some of the tourists want.

They don't know it, but they also are getting a glimpse of what the war has really done to Sri Lanka. More than 15,000 children, some as young as 8 years old, now sell sex on the southern beaches. Any one of them likely will have been shipped from the northern war zone—only about 100 miles away—by agents of a child-procuring mafia that preys on shattered homes. A family whose father has been killed in battle or whose mother has emigrated in search of work is an easy mark. Survivors will often accept a $100 "recruitment" fee from procurers posing as charitable workers looking for children to educate. The children themselves become everyday commodities in the war economy that now dominates what can only be called a war society. Plenty of other conflicts get more space on the world's front pages, but nowhere has war embedded itself more malignantly into the normal workings of a nation. Sri Lanka "hasn't been torn by war," says women's rights advocate Radhika Coomaraswamy, "it's been shredded."

It has now been 19 years since the Liberation Tigers of Tamil Eelam launched their war for an independent Tamil homeland in northern Sri Lanka. If war is hell, a war stalemated for so long deserves its own special ring of fire. In a country of 18 million people, 50,000 have died so far, an additional 30,000 have "disappeared" and more than 1 million have lost their homes. The social stresses are not as easy to quantify, but violent crime, especially rape, is rising rapidly. Sri Lanka also has the world's highest suicide rate; more Sri Lankans kill themselves each year—about 7,000—than are killed in the war. The depression and alcoholism that lead to most suicides must go largely untreated, as the nation's psychiatrists have joined the tens of thousands of other professionals who have fled abroad. More Sri Lankan psychiatrists now practice in London than in the whole of Sri Lanka, where only 18 remain.

The war's billion-dollar-a-year cost has stunted the economy and kept foreign investors away. Sri Lanka should have the greatest promise of any South Asian nation. It has the highest literacy rate in the region, no deep-rooted poverty, spectacular natural and archeological attractions for tourists, great deep-water ports lying along major shipping routes and lucrative natural resources of tea, gems and minerals. But the war has relentlessly ground down the nation's aspirations. People now accept 5 percent annual economic growth rather than reaching for twice that rate, says Saman Kelegama of the Institute of Policy Studies. "We're like someone with a gangrenous foot who leaves it to rot because it won't kill him tomorrow," he says. "The war is our gangrene and we live with it, rather than embarking on the radical surgery of ending it."

Numbers alone can't capture the social costs of the war of attrition. As in Vietnam 30 years ago, the government clings grimly to its fortified positions while the Tiger guerrillas stage hit-and-run raids from the jungle. Few prisoners are taken, and casualties can be horrific; in just two actions last year, the Tigers overran government-held towns and killed 3,000 soldiers. Nobody knows how many Tigers die, as many of their bodies are left to rot in the jungle after government bombing and shelling attacks. What's clear is that Sri Lanka is losing huge numbers of young men in the carnage. These include the guerrillas and troops who have died, as well as men who have fled the country to escape the war.

As a consequence, young unmarried women—tens of thousands of war widows among them—now outnumber available men by as many as 5 to 1 in northern war areas, according to one reasonable estimate. The imbalance is so great that a provincial government minister has suggested that polygamy be legalized. The idea is a nonstarter in a country where most people are strictly monogamist Buddhists, but the problem remains. Lacking husbands as well as jobs, almost 1 million Sri Lankan women have had to leave their country to find menial jobs as maids abroad, mainly in the Arab gulf countries.

The war continues to absorb Sri Lanka's men as they come of age. The Tigers take their recruits young and often forcibly. The government Army, though it is a volunteer force, can be just as difficult to resist. In a society wasted by war, only the Army offers a future to many impoverished young men. "It's a regular income and a rise in status you couldn't get any other way," says Tyrol Ferdinands, head of an antiwar group. A foot soldier's $57 monthly pay—$145 in the combat zone—is a huge incentive. Even death benefits are important to poor families who send their sons to war. A widow receives a lump sum of $2,173 if her husband comes back dead, plus his monthly pay to what would have been his retirement age of 55.

Living with this social rot has indeed become normal. While the war chews up poor, young Sri Lankans in the north, the southern elite in and around the capital, Colombo, have had to put up with no more than the occasional terrorist bomb. Ferdinands, general secretary of the National Peace Council of Sri Lanka, has been pressing for negotiations between the warring sides for years. His group has even sent envoys to Northern Ireland and South Africa to search for peacemaking ideas. But so far, the occasional talks between the Tigers and government negotiators have come to nothing. Only half-joking, Ferdinands suggests that the country subject all men of fighting age to a military draft. "Bring in conscription tomorrow and the war will end a few days later," he says, "when the first doctors, businessmen and stockbrokers lose their sons."

Army veteran Upali Ekanayake, 29, belongs to none of these categories. The son of a rural farming family, Ekanayake lives with other disabled veterans in Ranavirugama, "The Village of the War Heroes," secluded in a forest outside Colombo. Growing up near the war zone, Ekanayake says, he never wanted to be anything but a soldier. That career ended when a Tiger sniper shot him in the spine, leaving him paralyzed from the waist down.

Ekanayake still has his pride, as well as a young wife, Pushpa, who married him after his wound despite great parental opposition. Now he wants nothing more than peace. The Tamils should be refused full independence, he argues, but given autonomy in the north. "We have to end this war, and we have to go to any lengths to stop the fighting," Ekanayake says. "Otherwise this country will be filled with people in wheelchairs like me." That would make the wheelchair one more tool of everyday life in a war society.

ORGANIZATIONS TO CONTACT

The editors have compiled the following list of organizations concerned with the issues presented in this book. The descriptions are derived from materials provided by the organizations. All have publications or information available for interested readers. The list was compiled on the date of publication of the present volume; the information provided here may change. Be aware that many organizations take several weeks or longer to respond to inquiries, so allow as much time as possible.

Amnesty International
600 Pennsylvania Ave. SE, 5th Fl., Washington, DC 20003
(202) 544-0200 • fax: (202) 546-7142
e-mail: aiusamaro@igc.apc.org • website: http://www.amnesty-usa.org

Amnesty International is a grassroots activist organization that works to protect and preserve human rights. The organization is dedicated to the release of all prisoners of conscience, fair and prompt trials for political prisoners, the abolishment of the death penalty, and the cessation of torture, political killings, and "disappearances." Its publications include the annual *Amnesty International Report* and reports concerning ethnic violence and other human rights issues in individual countries.

Center for International Development and Conflict Management (CIDCM)
University of Maryland, College Park, MD 20742-7231
(301) 314-7703 • fax: (301) 314-9256
website: http://www.bsos.umd.edu/cidcm

CIDCM focuses on research, policy outreach, and linking development with conflict management. The scholars involved with the center are experts on issues of conflict management and resolution, economic development, human rights, ethics, and religious tolerance. CIDCM works closely with policymakers, nongovernment organizations, grassroot activists, and other groups. In addition to a variety of publications, CIDCM offers public lectures, academic courses, human rights education, mentoring, and internship programs.

Center for World Indigenous Studies (CWIS)
1001 Cooper Point Rd. SW, Suite 140-214, Olympia, WA 98502
(888) 286-2947
e-mail: jburrows@halycon.com • website: http://www.halcyon.com

CWIS is an independent research and education organization that concentrates on the political, social, and economic status of indigenous peoples. It publishes and distributes literature by people of Fourth World Nations, serves as a clearinghouse of ideas, and conducts conflict-resolution symposia and conferences. CWIS publishes the biannual online *Fourth World Journal*, the monthly newsletter *Fourth World Eyes*, and numerous papers, such as "Ireland, England, and the Question of Northern Ireland."

Derechos Human Rights
PO Box 2516, El Cerrito, CA 94530-5516
(510) 528-7794 • fax: (510) 526-4406
e-mail: hr@derechos.org • website: http://www.derechos.org

Derechos Human Rights promotes human rights worldwide by distributing human rights information, educating the public, providing support to local human rights organizations, and working to unmask human rights violators. Its publications include the online journal *Ko'aga Roñe'eta* and the newsletter *Without Impunity*.

The Fund for Peace
1701 K St. NW, 11th Fl., Washington, DC 20006
(202) 223-7940 • fax: (202) 223-7947
e-mail: Comments@fundforpeace.org • website: http://www.fundforpeace.org

The Fund for Peace promotes education and research on global problems that threaten human survival and proposes practical solutions to these problems. The organization publishes a number of publications on different international issues. Its publications concerning ethnic conflict and ethnic violence include "State Collapse and Ethnic Violence: Toward a Predictive Model."

Human Rights Watch (HRW)
350 Fifth Ave., 34th Fl., New York, NY 10018-3299
(212) 290-4700 • fax: (212) 736-1300
e-mail: hrwnyc@hwr.org • website: http://www.hrw.org

HRW is an international organization committed to defending human rights. It works to prevent discrimination, uphold political freedom, protect people from inhumane conduct during time of war, and bring offenders to justice. HRW publishes a broad spectrum of reports on issues related to ethnic violence, such as "Croatia: Second Class Citizens–The Serbs of Croatia," and "Leave None to Tell the Story: The Genocide in Rwanda." HRW also publishes the annual *World Report*.

Institute on Global Conflict and Cooperation (IGCC)
9500 Gilman Dr., Mail Code 0518
University of California at San Diego, La Jolla, CA 92093-0518
(619) 534-3352 • fax: (619) 534-7655
e-mail: ph13@sdcc12.ucsd.edu • website: http://www-igcc.ucsd.edu

IGCC studies the causes of international conflict and helps devise options for resolving conflict through international cooperation. The institute is committed to educating the next generation of international problem-solvers and peacemakers through research and teaching activities. It publishes the biannual *IGCC Newsletter* and numerous policy papers and briefs, including "Preventative Diplomacy and Ethnic Conflict: Possible, Difficult, Necessary" and "Ethnic Conflict and International Intervention."

International Crisis Group (ICG)
1522 K St. NW, Suite 822, Washington, DC 20005
(202) 986-9750 • fax: (202) 986-9751
e-mail: icg@his.com • website: http://www.intl-crisis-group.org

Headquartered in Brussels, Belgium, ICG is committed to strengthening the ability of the international community to understand and respond to impending crises. The organization, which focuses on field research and advocacy, works closely with governments and the media to bring important issues to the forefront and to provoke discussion of possible policy responses. ICG publishes the *ICG Annual Review* and diverse reports, including "Bosnia: Minority Return or Mass Relocation?" and "War in the Balkans: Consequences of the Kosovo Conflict and Future Options for Kosovo and the Region."

Project on Ethnic Relations (PER)
15 Chambers St., Princeton, NJ 08542-3718
(609) 683-5666 • fax: (609) 683-5888
e-mail: ethic@compuserve.com
website: http://www.netcom.com/~ethnic/per.html

PER is dedicated to reducing interethnic conflict in Central and Eastern Europe and the former Soviet Union. PER conducts programs of action, education, and research in these regions. Among its publications are an ethnic-relations bibliography and the quarterly *Bulletin* of project activities and regional events.

Search for Common Ground
1601 Connecticut Ave. NW, Suite 200, Washington, DC 20009
(202) 265-4300 • fax: (202) 232-6718
e-mail: search@sfcg.org • website: http://www.sfcg.org/default.htm

Search for Common Ground advocates the use of cooperative solutions to deal with conflict. The organization serves as a mediator in conflict situations, sponsors overseas centers that build conflict-resolution skills, provides courses and training in conflict resolution in schools in various countries, and sponsors forums, roundtables, and joint action projects. It also produces television programs and peace-oriented radio shows. Among its many publications are the book *Common Ground on Iraq-Kuwait Reconciliation*, the paper "Common Ground on Jordan-Israel-Palestine Trilateral Relations," the project report "Reporting Macedonia: The New Accommodation," and the quarterly *Search for Common Ground Newsletter*.

United States Institute of Peace
1200 17th St. NW, Suite 200, Washington, DC 20036-3011
(202) 457-1700 • fax: (202) 429-6063
e-mail: usip_requests@usip.org • website: http://www.usip.org

An independent, nonpartisan federal institution, the United States Institute of Peace promotes the peaceful resolution of international conflicts. One of its primary objectives is to educate the public about international conflicts and peacemaking efforts through publications, electronic outreach, workshops, and conferences. The institute also conducts research and trains international professionals in conflict management and resolution techniques, mediation, and negotiation skills. Its publications include the bimonthly newsletter *Peace Watch*, the reports "Rwanda: Accountability for War Crimes and Genocide" and "Kosovo Dialogue: Too Little, Too Late," and the books *NATO Transformed* and *Coercive Inducement.*

U.S. Committee for Refugees (USCR)
1717 Massachusetts Ave. NW, Suite 200, Washington, DC 20036
(202) 347-3507 • fax: (202) 347-3418
e-mail: uscr@irsa-uscr.org • website: http://www.refugees.org

USCR works to protect and assist refugees worldwide, including those fleeing from ethnic violence. It also documents and reports conditions faced by refugees, displaced persons, and people seeking asylum. The committee publishes the annual *USCR World Refugee Survey*, monthly refugee reports, and issue papers such as "Conflict and Displacement in Sri Lanka" and "Life After Death: Suspicion and Reintegration in Post-Genocide Rwanda."

BIBLIOGRAPHY

Books

Deborah Able	*Hate Groups*. Springfield, NJ: Enslow, 1995.
Gregory Alan-Williams	*A Gathering of Heroes: Reflections on Rage and Responsibility: A Memoir of the Los Angeles Riots.* Chicago: Academy Chicago, 1994.
Peter Balakian	*Black Dog of Fate: A Memoir.* New York: Broadway Books, 1997.
Susan Banfield	*Ethnic Conflicts in Schools.* Springfield, NJ: Enslow, 1995.
Ian J. Bickerton and Carla L. Klausner	*A Concise History of the Arab-Israeli Conflict.* Englewood Cliffs, NJ: Prentice Hall, 1998.
David Callahan	*Unwinnable Wars: American Power and Ethnic Conflict.* New York: Hill and Wang, 1997.
Jim Carnes	*Us and Them: A History of Intolerance in America.* New York: Oxford University Press, 1996.
Roselle K. Chartock and Jack Spencer, eds.	*Can It Happen Again? Chronicles of the Holocaust.* New York: Black Dog & Leventhal, 1995.
Ward Churchill	*A Little Matter of Genocide: Holocaust and Denial in the Americas, 1492 to the Present.* San Francisco: City Lights Books, 1997.
Charles Freeman	*Crisis in Rwanda.* Austin, TX: Raintree Steck-Vaughn, 1999.
Philip Gourevitch	*We Wish to Inform You that Tomorrow We Will Be Killed with Our Families: Stories from Rwanda.* New York: Farrar, Straus and Giroux, 1998.
Nathaniel Harris	*The War in Former Yugoslavia.* Austin, TX: Raintree Steck-Vaughn, 1998.
James A. Haught	*Holy Hatred.* Amherst, NY: Prometheus Books, 1995.
Michael Ignatieff	*The Warrior's Honor: Ethnic War and the Modern Conscience.* New York: Metropolitan Books, 1998.
Peter Janke, ed.	*Ethnic and Religious Conflicts: Europe and Asia.* Hants, England: Aldershot, 1994.
Arthur Jay Klinghoffer	*The International Dimension of Genocide in Rwanda.* New York: New York University Press, 1998.
Jay Robert Nash	*Terrorism in the 20th Century: A Narrative Encyclopedia from the Anarchists Through the Weathermen to the Unabomber.* New York: M. Evans, 1998.
Elaine Pascoe	*Racial Prejudice: Why Can't We Overcome?* New York: Franklin Watts, 1997.
Peter Taylor	*Behind the Mask: The IRA and Sinn Fein.* New York: TV Books, 1997.

Vamik D. Volkan   *Bloodlines: From Ethnic Pride to Ethnic Terrorism.* New
                        York: Farrar, Straus and Giroux, 1997.

Periodicals

Omer Bartov   "Defining Enemies, Making Victims: Germans, Jews,
                        and the Holocaust," *American Historical Review,* June
                        1998. Available from the American Historical
                        Association, Indiana University, 914 Atwater Ave.,
                        Bloomington, IN 47401.

John R. Bowen   "Ethnic Conflict: Challenging the Myths," *Current,*
                        January 1997.

Justin Brown   "A Serb and the Kosovo He Once Knew," *Christian
                        Science Monitor,* March 19, 1999.

Jamie Byrd   "Hate Kills," *Seventeen,* June 1999.

Scott Carrier   "A Himalayan Hell," *Esquire,* January 1999.

Lynne Duke   "Violence Grips Eastern Congo," *Washington Post,*
                        October 10, 1997.

Economist   "Ethnic Cleansing: Blood and Earth," September 23,
                        1995.

Economist   "Race Relations: The Riot that Never Was," April 24,
                        1999.

Amitai Etzioni   "'Kristallnacht' Remembered: History and Communal
                        Responsibility," *Commonweal,* February 12, 1999.

Michael J. Farrell   "Northern Ireland Memoir," *National Catholic Reporter,*
                        November 13, 1998. Available from 115 E. Armour
                        Blvd., Kansas City, MO 64111.

Ian Fisher   "Hutu and Tutsi Ask: Is a Unified Rwanda Possible?"
                        New York Times, April 6, 1999.

Steve Forbes   "Kosovo," *Forbes,* September 7, 1998.

Denise Gordon   "A Nation Struggles to Heal: April Marks the
                        Anniversary of 1994's Genocidal War in Rwanda,"
                        Essence, April 1998.

Michael R. Gordon   "Russian Jews Edgy as Country's Chaos Creates Ugly
                        Mood," *New York Times,* March 9, 1999.

Philip Gourevitch   "Waking Up to the Next War," *New Yorker,* October 26,
                        1998.

Hurst Hannum   "The Specter of Secession: Responding to Claims for
                        Ethnic Self-Determination," *Foreign Affairs,*
                        March/April 1998.

Sebastian Junger   "Kosovo's Valley of Death," *Vanity Fair,* July 1998.

Mark Landler   "In Indonesia, New Freedom Feeds Ethnic Friction,"
                        New York Times, May 21, 1998.

Mutuma Mathiu   "The Kurds Against the World," *World Press Review,*
                        May 1999.

Terry McCarthy   "Indonesia: Balkans of the East?" *Time,* June 7, 1999.

| Joe McNally and Kenneth Miller | "When the Shooting Stops," *Life,* January 1997. |

Andrew Meier — "Moscow Dispatch: HATEFUL," *New Republic,* March 29, 1999.

Seth Mydans — "Ancient Hatreds, New Battles," *New York Times Magazine,* March 14, 1999.

John O'Sullivan — "Black and Blue: New York Erupts over a Race-Tinged Killing—Again," *National Review,* April 19, 1999.

Annie Murphy Paul — "Psychology's Own Peace Corps," *Psychology Today,* July/August 1998.

Daniel Pearl — "Why Ethnic Cleansing, Once Under Way, Is So Difficult to Reverse," *Wall Street Journal,* April 22, 1999.

David Rohde — "Macedonia Village Typifies: (a) Peaceful Coexistence (b) Dormant Hatred," *New York Times,* May 30, 1999.

Greg Steinmetz — "Hitler's Heirs: German Skinhead Tells Court, 'I Am a Racist,' as Neo-Nazis Spread," *Wall Street Journal,* August 3, 1998.

Time — "A Life for a Life: As America Watches, a Texas Town Searches for Racial Healing After a Grisly Murder Trial," March 8, 1999.

Louise Tunbridge — "Burundi's 3-Year 'Campaign of Terror' Leaves a Bloody Trail on Its Campuses: Ethnic Conflict Leads to Violent Encounters Between Hutu and Tutsi Students," *Chronicle of Higher Education,* August 16, 1996. Available from 1255 23rd St. NW, Washington, DC 20037.

INDEX